Developing a Dynamic

DRAMA
MINISTRY

D1275318

Developing a Dynamic

DRAMA MINISTRY

Richard Major

Standard Publishing
Cincinnati, Ohio

The Standard Publishing Company, Cincinnati, Ohio
A division of Standex International Corporation
© 1999 by Richard Major
All rights reserved
Printed in the United States of America

06   05   04   03   02   01   00   99   5   4   3   2   1

Designed by Steve Diggs & Friends
Project Editor: Lise Caldwell
Typographic layout: Dale Meyers

Library of Congress Cataloging-in-Publication Data
Major, Richard, 1953-
      Developing a dynamic drama ministry / Richard Major.
         p.   cm.
      Includes bibliographical references.
      ISBN 0-7847-0915-7
      1. Drama in public worship.   I. Title.
BV289.M34   1999   98-31323
246'.72—dc21   CIP

For Karen, Will, and Shannon

Table of Contents

Many congregations are rediscovering the great spiritual and emotional impact that drama can have in enhancing a worship experience. The use of the fine arts in church can help provide a wholesome, meaningful fellowship time for the entire church family. In an age where it is increasingly difficult to find activities to positively influence the lives of families in the church, arts experiences provide a creative outlet for a church's congregation and help focus the energies of those involved in a communal way to bring glory to our Lord Jesus Christ.

This book is designed as a step-by-step approach to assist you in developing a dynamic drama ministry in your congregation. I draw on a variety of resources to provide a model that works not only within a church structure, but in the many other venues where I have performed, produced, or directed plays. Taking on the responsibility of organizing a drama ministry for your congregation or overseeing a production can be quite a humbling experience; you can easily feel overwhelmed and uncertain of the result. But the eternal optimist within me is confident that the fruits of your labors will be properly blessed if your heart, soul, and mind are in the right place. Offering your talents to God is an enriching, stimulating experience. When coupled with the dedicated efforts of many people, the results can be staggering.

So take it a step at a time! Reread portions of the book that seem simple at first, but when applied are more difficult. Do not be afraid to learn from your mistakes. Try not to be blind to the moments of pure brilliance that can occur spontaneously in the rehearsal process. After you get your feet wet, you may be surprised that the desire to create "something out of nothing" has found its place within you! You may find yourself wanting another opportunity to creatively present worthwhile ideas to your congregation in dramatic form. You may be equally surprised to learn you have grown spiritually through the artistic process.

So as I tell my students: "Sit back, relax, laugh (and cry) to your heart's content; a formidable task lies ahead!"

Please note that for the sake of consistency, I have used masculine pronouns throughout the book. However, terms such as actor, director, producer, and stage manager can refer to a man or a woman.

I wish to thank my dear friend, Dr. Paul Blowers of the Emmanuel School of Religion, Dr. Bruce Shields, also of Emmanuel, and my friends and colleagues at Milligan College, especially Dr. Lee Magness for his encouragement in the writing of this book. I also wish to express my gratitude to Missy Luce and Kristie Rolape for their assistance in research tasks. A special thank you to my parents, Charles and Frances Major, my family, and the good folks at Dry Run Christian Church in West Portsmouth, Ohio, who gave me many opportunities as a child and young adult to perform in the dramatic productions that eventually led to my choosing theater as a vocation for life. Thank you to my good friends at Hopwood Memorial Christian Church for the many occasions we have had to perform together. Lastly, to my editor, Lise Caldwell, I extend a very grateful thank you, for her suggestions, patience, and ideas (and did I mention patience?) in seeing me through the writing process.

Richard Major
November 1998

Getting Your Feet on the Ground

*A*s every man hath received the gift,

even so minister the same one to another,

as good stewards of the manifold grace of God.

1 Peter 4:10

Getting Your Feet on the Ground

Defining Your Purpose

The very first step in establishing a drama ministry for your congregation should be defining your overall purpose for wanting drama in your church. Is it simply to serve a segment of your congregation? Or will the establishment of such a ministry have the potential to reach a greater constituency and, in the process, enhance the worship experiences you already have firmly in place? Defining the purpose of drama in your particular congregation will ultimately help you decide exactly what you want to do with drama. Perhaps you want to present a dramatic interpretation of the Bible. Or you want to use sketches or skits to announce an upcoming church event. Or maybe you want to help people better understand what God's message is for them in a very personal way. Whatever your primary objective may be, using drama as a ministry in your congregation can be a refreshing new way to present significant social issues or ideas for strengthening one's spiritual life. Drama also can be used to help us understand our relationships with other Christians and to grapple with events in our lives that compel us to live more faithfully. At the outset, a drama ministry team must have a clearly defined answer to this question: Why use drama?

Drama is intrinsic to life. When we tell a story, we cannot help but be dramatic. When someone recounts a personal life story, whether it is humorous or tragic, something about the story compels us to listen. Think of your own experiences listening to the many stories told to you by family members or dear friends. While you may initially wince at hearing the story for the one-thousandth time, the really good stories are ones that we can hear over and over and still enjoy. A marvelous teller will relate a story as though it is completely new and spontaneous. Really good stories often are embellished from teller to teller, each person finding his own way to uniquely relate the drama of the story. When words are spoken *and* acted out, there is an impact which can be felt. The emotional appeal of art can touch lives in amazing ways.

The Bible is the ultimate script for life. Like a good play, it holds many dramatic possibilities. The Bible narrative can be very exciting. The Bible provides all the dramatic conventions of plot, setting, character development, dialogue or language, thought, climax, and even spectacle.

Life lessons are all over the Bible, from the creation story and Adam and Eve, to the prophesy of Hosea, the stories of David and Job, to the Gospels and beyond. Whether on its own or used in conjunction with music, Scripture, sermon, or multimedia presentation, drama can have a lasting effect on a congregation. Perhaps your drama ministry team will want to integrate drama into the weekly worship service before tackling larger productions that might include celebrations of Christmas, the Easter season, or other special occasions. Thinking of creative ways to plug into the existing seasonal themes of services should help the team with its development.

Key to the endeavor is the careful and cautious planning your team will need when implementing and incorporating drama into the worship experience. The most effective use of drama in worship occurs when it works harmoniously with the other elements of a worship service. Planning with the worship team and platform leaders is essential to maximize the overall effect of the entire service. While coordinating these efforts takes time and patience, preparing in this way will give the service just the climactic build you are trying to achieve. Working too independently of one another may result in sending a mixed or unclear message to your congregation. Whether you are doing a choral interpretation of a Scripture passage, or dramatizing the theme of your minister's sermon, the use of drama can have a profound effect on your congregation. The point is to work and plan together. Try to leave nothing to chance. Imagine together how incorporating these experiences for your congregation in your worship services will bring glory and honor to God. Remember, in this case the right hand *does* need to know what the left hand is doing.

In summary, your drama team should spend some quality time together articulating reasons for wanting to establish a team in the first place. Such prayerful meeting will provide a firm foundation for the group when setting this venture in motion. This reflective time will also serve as a way of delineating the reasons why drama should be used in worship services. Do not add drama to your worship service merely because it is the current trend. Investigate the advantages of integrating drama into your services. List the potential gains of, and develop specific purposes for, your drama ministry. This will go a long way in helping the group win over any potential naysayer who resists change.

Identifying the Need Within Your Church

There is a very good chance that your congregation has some form of drama already in place. Perhaps it is an annual pageant for the Christmas or Easter season. Or maybe your youth group produces dramatic sketches or skits to comment on some significant relevant social issues. Just maybe your congregation has used these seasonal opportunities to find an alternative form of providing a worthwhile worshipful experience for the congregation. What I propose is that such fare become a staple in the church experience and not just a single or biannual frolic or novelty.

Many congregations are looking for more meaningful ways to explore and study the Bible, to grapple with relevant social issues, or deal with the difficult questions that arise in the Christian life. The use of drama can be an explosive and unique way to deal with these pertinent issues. Drama can help stir a congregation to action if it is done well. The church has long embraced the use of music to celebrate and praise God. Likewise, a well planned and executed dramatic sketch can be a powerful tool to convey the message of Jesus Christ. Often, however, drama is added as an afterthought, with little time devoted to polishing the end product. This is usually ineffective and often detrimental. With systematic work, drama can unleash the energy of the creative spirit in inspiring ways.

Establishing a Relationship With Other "Platform" People

The question remains: "How do we integrate drama into the worship service?" The answer will likely be as varied as the congregations we seek to serve. While some congregations may resist change, others are very open to the idea of integrating drama into the weekly format of their worship service. My suggestion is to work as closely with the worship team, other platform personnel, and the church board, as possible. People generally do not like surprises, especially in their worship services, so plan cautiously and prayerfully before making any changes in the way you currently do things in your Sunday service.

Integrating drama into the worship experience will require time and patience. Just as the church choir or praise band must rehearse before performing for a Sunday morning service, a drama team will have to plan and rehearse as well. It will take tremendous organization, management, and a productive period of time devoted to rehearsing. So take your time, but try not to be intimidated by the task you undertake.

Before embarking on developing a drama ministry in your congregation, iate ministers, your worship leader, the _____ of music, and your church board. These individuals will help your team define goals and objectives about what will be most beneficial to your congregation. Establishing a good working relationship with these individuals will help ensure success. Simple courtesies such as not coming on too strong, and remembering that ultimately we are using all of these experiences to glorify God, will make the link in the chain more stable. The last thing you want to do is upset the orderly flow of how programs are planned for the church.

Integral to the success of using drama in your church experience is gaining the approval and support of your congregation. I suggest you do this systematically, respecting the "chain of command" within your congregation. Getting the support of the minister and other platform people will help you achieve your goals. Do your very best to seek out other groups within the church who may need to approve your drama ministry. Meet with your elders, outreach committee members, or anyone else within your congregation who can offer you guidance and support. Be open to their suggestions as you plan how to integrate drama experiences into the worship service. Try to be sensitive to the needs and desires of your entire congregation, and not just one segment of it.

Consider providing the entertainment for a non-Sunday morning church event, such as a dinner or banquet or even for the mid-week service, before embarking on integrating drama into the weekly worship service. Such occasions will enable your group to gain experience and confidence in organizing material for presentation. Once this groundwork is carefully laid, the group may be ready to integrate drama into the Sunday morning worship experience.

One simple, yet unique way to begin is to take on the responsibilities of reading the Scripture each Sunday. Working with your minister, worship team, and other platform leaders can make this an exciting preliminary opportunity for your drama ministry team. This is also a particularly interesting way to test the "dramatic waters" of your congregation. Initially it may be as simple as thoroughly rehearsing a passage of Scripture and finding specific points of emphasis to enhance the understanding of the text. Within a short time your group could stage simple choral readings of Scripture for the worship service. Such work can help your team become recognized as a vital contributor to each week's service.

While there are obviously many different contemporary translations of the Bible that could be used for these purposes, one need not necessarily look any further than the King James or Revised Standard Versions of the Bible to find ways to take the Scripture apart and divide it among two to five readers. There is a dramatized version of the New Testament now available, edited by Michael Perry (and published by Zondervan), that does this for you. This is such a simple way to add a little sparkle and creativity to the reading of Scripture. The listener is more likely to really *hear* the content of the passage when the material is presented in this way. The fact that the passage has been rehearsed by the team presenting it also ensures a certain amount of success.

Unfortunately, most people assigned to reading Scripture for a service probably spend no more than a few minutes reviewing the text before they read it aloud for the congregation. A team of readers is more likely to rehearse and work through the assigned reading or Scripture a few times before presenting it in a service. The leader can direct the reading in a way that taps into your group's special talents to emphasize portions of the text that will aid the congregation's understanding of the passage.

Most translations of the Bible lend themselves very well to choral reading. Generally someone should be assigned the role of narrator. The narrator may read the non-dialogue portion of the text. Depending on the passage, there may be other identifiable "characters" in the text, such as one or more of the disciples or Jesus in New Testament Scripture, or a prophet in an Old Testament passage. Once your actors have become adept at doing this type of reading, they may want to experiment with adding music to the presentation. Many churches have members who play stringed or wind instruments that would provide great accompaniment to the reading of a passage of Scripture.

Again, this gradual integration of drama into the framework of what is normally done in worship will help your group to be accepted by the congregation. I have often been greatly surprised by the results of using this very simple innovation in the Scripture reading portion of a service. When done properly, with as little as an hour of rehearsal, the words in a given text can come alive for the listener.

Strategies for Success

Think for a moment. Besides reading the Scripture and staging choral readings, what are some other ways that drama can slowly be woven into the fabric of the weekly worship experience? Consider using drama to make announcements during the service. Though there is the risk that this device can become "cute" or trivialize the serious intent of your group's ministry, it may help your team be more readily accepted by the congregation. Besides, this opportunity will enable your group to experiment with its comedic potential. "Announcement drama" also allows your group to experiment with writing original material, which is a vital link to your group's continued success. By putting together a "special announcement" sketch, your team will learn some fundamental concepts about how to connect with an audience. While the result may be comedic, I suggest that considerable time be given to rehearsing the sketch before performing it for the congregation. I've had some great ideas that when staged, failed miserably. So please give yourself ample time to rehearse. Once your group has more experience, it may not need as much time to prepare for these sketches, but should initially approach them with disciplined rehearsal. Who knows, a special "character" may come from doing this type of work, one that can become a periodic staple to the announcement process.

Actually, I think finding a way for your group to do some of this kind of original sketch material may help in recruiting others to be a part of your team. I think the entire emotional impact of what a drama ministry has to offer needs to be explored by your team's membership. Humor is a significant part of the human experience and has as much validity as any other emotion. To me, it is very gratifying to find a way to make people consider something I think is important, while also helping them find ways to laugh at themselves. For many years I have directed plays that are geared to young audiences and families. Sometimes the themes of the plays are very serious. What I always try to find, though, is a way to make the play funny to the children as well as the adults. As adults we need to remember the child that lives within all of us. If we can learn how to successfully make something so simple a young child can understand it, while keeping the adults connected to our work on another level of understanding, then we have truly learned something significant about how an audience reacts and responds to our dramatic work.

The human spirit is as unique as it is varied, yet there are universal themes and experiences that bind us together. The tragedy of losing someone or something close to us, the humor of certain life situations we all share, the appreciation we have for those who have an impact on our lives, are just a sampling of experiences that link us together as human beings. Drama explores the full gamut of the emotions, thoughts, and experiences we share with one another. For the Christian, it is a marvelous opportunity to express one's faith and to passionately engage in praising God.

Another avenue is performing in conjunction with the special services provided for children in your congregation. Performing for junior church may be a way to give your team some experience, and provides children with an opportunity to occasionally participate in sketches designed to educate and enrich their lives. Do not expect this to be any easier than preparing sketches for adults. In many ways performing for children is *more* difficult. Children will let you know immediately whether or not they like what is being presented. Embrace this challenge! I think if the performers can captivate a child's attention, then they will find performing for adults much easier. Someone may want to begin a drama ministry team specifically devoted to working for and with children. Involve the children in the sketch! Whether they are providing the sound effects of a storm, or playing animals in a reenactment of Noah and the ark, children should be allowed to participate. Most congregations are open to ideas that will successfully engage the children of the church, the older youth, or the many young single or married adults in their membership. Also remember that most parents will do virtually anything for their children. While some adults may be hesitant to perform in a drama team's ministry to other adults, they may get a real charge out of doing drama for the children of the congregation. The other thing to keep in mind is that this opportunity may also be quite attractive to senior members of your congregation. What a unique way to present the many wonderful life lessons from the Bible!

Getting children familiar with and enthusiastic about drama can also help with other dramatic projects your team may tackle in the future. Larger productions generally need actors of all ages. By providing more opportunities for the children of your congregation to see live theater, they will in turn be more apt to try it themselves in the future. For any aspiring actor, the challenges of performing for children are well worth the effort and the commitment. Nothing sounds better than children laughing, shouting out loud a "warning" to the actors, or collectively cheering the hero of the story. What an absolute thrill this is for the performer or director who brings these stories to life!

To summarize, it is important to lay the groundwork for a drama group in your church very meticulously. Present the idea of including drama in worship in the best way you can. Gain the support of the ministerial team, the worship leader, the church board, and other church staff who will help your group be a success. Find innovative ways to win over those who may resist change. Often one bad experience may spell doom for the future use of drama in your church, so it is very important to be as inclusive as possible. Find ways to win over potential naysayers, while keeping the excitement and enthusiasm of those supporting new ways to celebrate and glorify God. After laying the foundation very carefully, take it a step at a time to ensure the best possible results.

Who Are We Trying to Serve, Anyway?

And whatsoever ye do in word or deed,

do all in the name of the Lord Jesus,

giving thanks to God and the Father by him.

Colossians 3:17

Chapter 2

Who Are We Trying to Serve, Anyway?

A Brief History of Church Drama

The church has a very checkered history when it comes to the use of drama in services. Not much is known about the use of drama in early church history, but we do know that at some point the church began using theatrical presentations for the purposes of promoting the values of Christian faith and salvation through Jesus Christ. As early as A.D. 925, the church found a way to celebrate the resurrection of Jesus in an Easter service at the monastery of St. Gall in Switzerland. Four brethren costumed themselves in such a fashion as to act out the resurrection. Positioning themselves before the sepulcher, the brethren sang of Jesus' resurrection. The drama was completed by having all the congregation join in by singing. This early form of liturgical drama was known as a "trope." While the term "trope" originally was used to define a short musical melody, it eventually began to refer to a theatrical text that would be used to reenact a particular story from the Bible. Perhaps the most famous and most produced of these was the "Quem Quaeritis" trope which sought to enrich the congregation's faith through reenacting Jesus' resurrection. By A.D. 1000, this Easter dialogue was found throughout much of Western Europe.

It was during the height of the Middle Ages, though, that the use of drama to evangelize, convert, and educate the masses primarily took place. Thus, the medieval passion play emerged. The purpose of the passion play was to tell of the coming, birth, life, death, and resurrection of Jesus. Through acting out these stories, the masses were exposed to the basic tenets of the Christian life, because most people could not read the Bible for themselves. These plays were also known as the "cycle plays." Other plays that became popular during this period of time were the "miracle" or "mystery" plays. These plays would contain humorous characters and eventually garnered disdain among church officials. Most religious plays of the medieval period were directly related to particular celebrations of the church calendar.

By the mid-sixteenth century religious drama began to decline. Martin Luther (1483-1546) and his followers disliked plays primarily for the iconographic and sometimes disrespectful representation of Jesus. To add to the controversy, Luther was soon depicted in plays as a fool and thus drama was used as a religious weapon. Because of the whirl of controversy surrounding most religious plays of the time, authorities began to regulate and eventually ban plays altogether, even though plays were extremely popular with the public.

It is my opinion that once religious plays fell out of favor, drama in the church has never really recovered. We seem to live in an era that is almost devoid of good religious plays and of writers who are committed to writing plays or screenplays that have religious themes. In 1970, the musical *Godspell* hit the American stage, retelling the gospel of Jesus' ministry through Matthew's account. The show used a multitude of theatrical devices to bring the message of Jesus' life to a wider audience. This was right on the heels of the much more controversial *Jesus Christ Superstar*, a rock opera by Andrew Lloyd Webber and Tim Rice. *Godspell,* by Jon-Michael Tebelak, with music and lyrics by Stephen Schwartz, was popularly successful and gave many fledgling Christian drama troupes at the time a powerful medium to affect lives. As both a performer and a director of the musical *Godspell,* I can personally attest to the power and life-changing effect the play has had on me. This work, unlike any other I have ever been a part of, is particularly potent when performed by a cast of believers. It is vibrant, jubilant, and joyously expresses the hope that Jesus Christ conveys throughout the New Testament.

This raises some interesting questions given the fact that early religious plays, while popular with the viewing public, grew to be suspicious in the eyes of the church leadership. Christians justifiably feel uncomfortable when Christ is portrayed inappropriately. Therefore, be certain to respectfully represent the story of Jesus to the public while staying as faithful as possible to the account as we know it. Some feathers may be ruffled in the process, but I think as long as one truly respects the message, then the product as a whole will be acceptable unto God and powerful enough to impact the lives of both believers and unbelievers.

Recruiting Members of a Drama Team

First, identify the members of your congregation who seem to be open to new ideas. Look for the outgoing personalities that fill your pews on Sunday morning. Chances are that people who participate in the choir may enjoy participating in dramatic sketches. But for goodness sake, don't overlook those seemingly shy or quiet people who may be looking for a meaningful way to express themselves. Some of the best actors I've known and worked with are just these kind of people. They tend to feel much more at ease in front of an audience when they are portraying a character. Church members who are by vocation teachers, professionals, or display leadership capacities and performance abilities in other ways may also be good sources to contact. This could include young people who spend hours taking dance, acrobatic and gymnastic lessons, or young athletes who excel on the baseball diamond, basketball or volleyball court, or the football field.

Central to the idea of recruiting people to the drama ministry team should be the decision about whether or not this group will be performing weekly, biweekly, monthly, quarterly, or preparing for a larger production that may be centered around an Easter or Christmas theme. If your team is planning to integrate drama into the worship service on a regular basis, then it is imperative the team members be caring, committed actors who will participate in and support an ongoing drama ministry. This is vastly different from the team that may oversee seasonal productions. The seasonal production may only require a six- to eight-week commitment, whereas an ongoing drama ministry is just that, requiring a considerable weekly devotion to the team throughout the entire year.

Full-scale productions have the appeal of involving larger segments of your congregation. While this may be a general goal or objective of your drama team's outreach, it is highly unlikely that your church will only be doing large-scale productions on a regular basis. This occasional involvement of participants in a broader way is very good and I will address these concerns later in this book. But the week-to-week work of keeping a drama ministry flourishing within your congregation and integrating the use of drama into the weekly service is something entirely different.

As I suggested earlier, build a team that is a good cross section of your congregation's membership. Once you have identified some prospective members, try to gauge where everyone is in regard to level of talent and experience. It is important to make those who want to be a part of this ministry feel as though they are making a contribution. Although formal auditions are one way to judge talent, an audition per se for a drama team ministry is probably not the format you'll want to use to form your team. Auditions can be intimidating to people, so identify potential members in a less daunting way. Strategies for holding auditions for particular parts in large-scale productions are discussed in Chapter 7.

Begin recruiting by advertising extensively in your church bulletin and through announcements for several weeks prior to meeting for the first time.

This will help ensure that those interested in drama ministry will be aware the team is forming. At the designated first meeting, be prepared to work with who you have. After meeting for a few weeks, those who are most committed will continue to come to the meetings, and those who are not as committed will more than likely weed themselves out. It would be wise for your group to decide on ways to invite new members to join the team a couple of designated times a year. This will give the team an opportunity to continue to grow and evolve. Another strategy may be to keep all meetings open to interested individuals with the understanding that new people will gradually be worked into the various sketches your group may be rehearsing or writing at the time. The bottom line is to trust your basic instincts when choosing the model that will work best for your team and your congregation.

It is important to remember that new members will more than likely emerge as talented, committed, responsible people who will want to be a part of this unique opportunity to serve your congregation. It has been my experience that while some coaxing may be warranted in recruiting viable members for your team, you shouldn't cajole or prod to the point of alienating someone in the process. You may begin with a rather small, but dedicated group of people. Remember, significant opportunities for creatively expressing one's faith in God can result from the fruitful labors of just a few people. Place the focus on that objective rather than trying to estimate your eventual success by the sheer number of people involved in the drama team's ministry.

Also, think beyond just the need for actors when recruiting members of a team. The real work of presenting any drama lies with the production team that helps pull the project off. Utilize the talents of carpenters, electricians, sound technicians, musicians, and seamstresses. They can help your team realize its true potential, especially in larger productions. Virtually everyone in the congregation may eventually contribute something, whether it is a prop, or expertise in using a computer to print flyers, or help creating some special effect for a presentation. So recruit a core group that you would like to see involved and then have a first meeting to begin forming the team.

Identifying Your Target Audience

Now that you have identified the potential members of a drama ministry for your church, the first question you may want to answer is: "Who is our audience?" Knowing your audience is important in everything that will follow, from script selection, through the casting and rehearsal process, to the finished product. The approach to the work is often dictated by your target audience.

Let's assume that the target audience is the adults of the congregation. Your group needs to then ask some very basic questions. "Who are the adults in our congregation?" "What are the general demographics of this group, such as age, size, socioeconomic makeup, race or ethnic makeup, education level, and occupations?" Answering these questions will enable your group to accommodate everyone in the congregation in the sketches your group will eventually prepare. The answers to these questions also will assist the group in making stylistic choices in the material it either selects or prepares for worship services. Is your congregation more formal or more laid back? Do they like innovation or are they more inclined to traditional approaches of integrating new things into the worship experience? Be sensitive to these very important questions. Undoubtedly, your success will hinge on how well you decipher and dissect the answers to these questions.

The next important sequence of questions are those relating to the relevant issues that are facing your congregation. This may have to do with issues of faith, service, stewardship, growth, or other spiritual matters. Again, sensitivity to these concerns will assist your team in making vital decisions in how best to serve your congregation. The group will then be ready to brainstorm the most effective means to reach the congregation. Begin these types of sessions by giving consideration to all ideas that are presented. Make a list and then weigh the merits of each idea. While some ideas may be too simple or not simple enough, the cataloging of generated ideas will help the group identify ways to implement its message. As I will write later in this book, ideas will come to you and the members of your team at highly unlikely times. I try to keep a pen and paper with me at all times to jot down ideas. I find that when I do this, I'm much more likely to remember to implement the idea than I am when I trust my memory to recall it later.

Another set of questions may be: "Will our team be comprised only of adults, only of young children, only of senior high and college youth, or will it be a mix of the congregation?" If you are performing for children, "Will it be children performing for other children, adults performing for children, or will it be a combination of talent?" Each group needs to decide what works best for its audience. A particular team may want to do some projects with adults only or children only, while occasionally doing a production that can use an intergenerational approach. Make the appropriate choices that best serve your congregation. I rather like the intergenerational model because we can all learn from one another. This extension of the family can be a positive experience for all involved. Each age group has a tendency to help break down some of the barriers that prevent effective communication across the age spectrum. This model, in my opinion, offers a marvelous opportunity for members of a congregation to grow closer to one another. However, if you are going to have a group that meets regularly to train actors, and a group that seeks to grow together spiritually, it may be best to limit the membership to adults only initially. As your team grows, and as you find yourself more confident and experienced, branching out to form separate groups among your congregation's youth and children may be an exciting outlet for your drama team's growing potential and ministry.

"Places, Please!" Organizing Your Drama Ministry

Everything should be done in a fitting

and orderly way.

1 Corinthians 14:40, *NIV*

Chapter 3
"Places, Please!" Organizing Your Drama Ministry

Monthly, Biweekly, or Weekly Meetings

People are perhaps busier these days than at any point in history. The struggle of dealing with career, family obligations, school activities, lessons for the children in dance, art, and music, or baseball, soccer, and basketball practice keeps the average person extraordinarily busy. Add to this seemingly never ending list the feeling that the world is open 24 hours a day, seven days a week, 365 days a year, and we all swirl in an abyss of scheduling. Thus, the first dilemma that any beginning drama group is going to encounter will be finding time for planning and regular meetings. Working with your group's tight schedules may pose some preliminary hurdles for everybody, but let's face it, this will also ultimately determine who most wants to be a part of this type of ministry and who does not. So don't be discouraged if a monthly meeting time is all you can arrange. The monthly meetings can successfully serve as actor training and team building time, or as planning meetings for upcoming performances and production.

As I've indicated throughout the book, meticulous planning must be a part of every successful performance that will be staged. As your group gets closer to actually performing, obviously meetings will need to occur more frequently, but initially once or twice a month may be enough. As with any meeting, set a time limit and try to always honor it. Insist that meetings begin on time, develop an agenda, and finish when you say they are going to. Why, you ask, is this important? I think it promotes a sincere respect for the "work" of the group. It also sends a signal for later on that the group will adhere to a tight time schedule in rehearsals as well. Nothing is worse than an open-ended rehearsal or meeting that seems to drag on forever. People just do not have the time to do this, and your group's success may hinge on this simple rule. On the other hand, your meetings need to be flexible enough to accommodate as many potential members as possible. So, you may want to meet two different times a month at times that accommodate the majority of those who would like to participate. Extra rehearsal for particular performers may be scheduled in addition to this time.

Once your group has done the preliminary work of writing goals and objectives through a mission statement, and after meeting and discussing these objectives with the congregation's ministerial personnel, take the time to allow team members to develop relationships with one another. I think each regular meeting should begin with a devotion, prayer, and sharing time for the team's members. This spiritual time together will allow the team to become closer to one another. It also serves as a reminder that the tasks which lie ahead are achievable, with God's help, through the collective work of the group.

In the early sessions you may also need to devote some time to training the actors. Educate them about basic terminology that will be used in rehearsal sessions. Take time to use some of the acting games and improvisations found in Chapter 4 and Appendix 3. Vocal or physical excercise may also be part of the regimen your group incorporates into the meetings.

I think such disciplined work will help the group unify more quickly and have the benefit of giving you a specific routine that will serve you well during large-scale productions. Warming up as an actor is similar to warming up as an athlete. For the latter it is important to have all of the physical muscles loosened and ready to go in order to achieve maximum performance level. With acting we also need to make sure the vocal instrument is ready to do what we'll need it to do for a particular character. By establishing a routine the entire group does together, you also develop a team mentality, in which everyone desires to do his best individually, but also strives to work together as an ensemble.

Your weekly sessions may include devoting some brainstorming time to upcoming events or performances, while allowing time for rehearsals that need to take place for more immediate performance dates. Early on the group must devise ways to constructively critique one another. A device I use in teaching is to have the individuals doing the sketch/scene be given the first opportunity to comment on their own work. I then solicit responses from the other members of the team, and lastly offer my own comments to the performers. Instruct the group to keep the responses honest, but positive and constructive. As director, try to comment on what you actually saw rather than what you didn't see. This will help the performers enhance what they're doing, and will serve as an encouragement rather than a discouragement to them.

One teaching device I use is to have different combinations of students perform the same scripted material. (This device was routinely used in my professional training as an actor.) The director blocks the scene, giving the actors their specific patterns of movement. All the actors write down the same blocking (instructions for movement on the stage). Everyone is assigned a partner with whom to initially rehearse the scene, then acting partners may be switched within the groups. Doing the same script and blocking with another acting partner helps keep the performance fresh and spontaneous. This is a very effective teaching tool for the beginner as well as the more advanced performer. The enjoyment here is derived from seeing the many possible interpretations of a given piece of text. By constantly changing the chemistry of the performers, actors can very effectively learn from one another. This delightful twist keeps a sketch buoyant and spontaneous, and will greatly assist the teacher or director who is trying to put together a more balanced performance.

Just for fun you may occasionally want to place actors in roles of the opposite sex. Sometimes gender-specific characterizations are needed to make a point in a particular sketch. Other times it may not really matter if a character is played by a male or female. This healthy experimentation may give your sketch another perspective for consideration. This technique may only be something you try in rehearsal, but then again it may open your eyes to a relevant and captivating way to eventually present the material. Trust your instincts in this regard, and you will make the right decision when the time comes to perform the script for your congregation.

The drama team's meetings need to be fun, but structured. Take breaks when needed, allowing the group to socialize, but do keep a goal in mind for each of your sessions. The leadership of the team needs to be able to find a good balance in how time is spent each week. If any real work is to be done, some structure is necessary.

Quarterly, Monthly, Biweekly, or Weekly Performances

Remember when I said the group should move slowly, even cautiously, in organizing themselves? I think this also should be the standard when deciding performance dates. Of course, much of this decision has to do with the type of script your group will be producing. While it may be easier to develop three-to-five-minute dramatic or humorous sketches that could be included in services on a weekly basis, my suggestion is to move slowly. You will not forward the cause of drama at your church if you try to perform when you do not allow for adequate rehearsal time. If your focus is on providing meaningful, brief dramas in conjunction with worship services, you may wish to initially plan to perform once a quarter or once a month. As you, your actors, and your church's leadership grow in skill and ability to make the most effective use of drama, increase the frequency.

If your group intends to focus on larger scale productions, you may not wish to plan for more than two a year, with perhaps smaller performances in between. Later I will discuss how to take such productions on the road, extending the life of the performance for your group.

With everyone's busy schedules, this is probably about all you will be able to handle unless your group has the advantage of a paid staff person whose main responsibility is to organize and develop drama ministry within the church. Do what is best for your group. As the group grows and expands, you may be able to routinely incorporate drama into some aspect of your weekly worship experience, be it Sunday morning or evening service. The bottom line is to be realistic and consider the individual schedules and commitments of your group members.

Establishing Goals for the Drama Team

Any effective group needs to establish general and specific goals for themselves. While much of the foundation for establishing goals will take place as the group defines its purpose and lays the groundwork by identifying the need within the church, it is probably still a good idea to write a mission statement for the group. The careful writing of this statement will outline what the group desires to accomplish. Having a clearly defined idea of how your minister and worship team intend to integrate drama into the weekly service will greatly aid your group in writing this statement. Try to be as specific as you possibly can as you define your goals and objectives. Review the previous notes you have made about your congregation's demographics and then evaluate your congregation's needs, goals, and objectives. Is your congregation community-minded, missions-minded, or more concerned with daily individual discipleship? Whatever the case, bathe your decisions in earnest prayer. This aspect of your development as a team is vital. Take as much time as you need to in order to accommodate the ideas, suggestions, goals, and objectives of your drama team's membership. This foundational step will be the solid rock upon which your team will be built, so carefully consider this in establishing your team.

Finding, Creating, and Selecting Appropriate Scripts

In Appendix 1 of this book, you will find a resource list of sources that provide skits, dramatic sketches, one-acts, and full-length religious plays. I have also included some World Wide Web sites that may help you see what some churches are doing with their drama ministry teams. The best source of performance material may be from within your own group. Creating your own scripts may be just the ticket to success in carrying out the goals you have established. Do not be intimidated by script writing, but do not be fooled into thinking it is an easy thing to do. While creating your own work can be very time consuming, the sense of sincere ownership of the production is rarely more gratifying than when a group has produced its own script. Begin with simple skits and dramatic sketches and consider moving toward full-fledged productions.

Inspiration for developing your own script may come from a variety of sources, including necessity. For example, your reading committee may not be able to find suitable scripted material for your group to perform. It may be simpler to devise your own script than to continue to search for just the right thing to produce. Again, my advice is to trust your own intuition. By writing your own script, you may be able to draw new potential members for your group: those who are interested in writing, but not necessarily interested in performing.

On the other hand, trying to generate "something out of nothing" may be too taxing for your newly-formed group. You do not want to undermine your own potential success by tackling too much. Use common sense to make your decision, and once the decision has been made, stick to it.

If you do find yourself creating your own scripts, be sure to remember to include other resource people such as your minister, music minister, or worship team into an ongoing discussion. For example, knowing a couple of weeks in advance that your preacher is planning a sermon topic that may be introduced by a sketch from the drama team can give your team a specific direction. That way, you are working within the structure of a planned worship service rather than on your own. Believe me, this makes the daunting task of creating a script much easier. If at all possible, perform the sketch for the minister beforehand. This collaborative effort will serve everyone better in the end. Who knows, by doing so, you may be able to give each other some ideas that can improve the performance. This is the common-sense approach I recommend for your team. Ultimately these collaborative efforts have the effect of making the integration of drama into the normal worship service more palatable to a wider segment of your congregation.

Drama within worship is most effectively used in conjunction with other elements of the service. If the correlation of a scene to the service is not apparent to the congregation, they may spend more time wondering "What did that have to do with anything?" than allowing it to open their hearts to a sermon, song, or Scripture. By discerning beforehand what the overall desired effect should be, your group will probably have a higher success rate.

Another way to create your own material is to reenact an event or parable from the Bible from a new point of view. I was once asked to do a sketch that would depict the familiar story of Jesus' birth, which included Mary's trip to Bethlehem on a donkey. I decided an interesting approach might be to tell the story from the donkey's viewpoint. Another time I helped devise a script that told the story from the point of view of a traveler who happened to get the last room at the inn before Mary and Joseph arrived seeking a place to stay. Choose original ideas that will have meaning and substance for your group. As your team continues to grow, and through your collaborative work with other Sunday morning worship leaders, you will undoubtedly discover other ways to make meaningful contributions to the worship experience.

If you do decide to create your own scripts and sketches, the following guidelines may be beneficial to you. First, brainstorm to generate possible ideas for your group to perform. I think it helps to jot these plot ideas down in skeletal form. Second, decide who the characters in the sketch are going to be. Then begin to flesh out the characters. Who are they? What do they want or need? How do they fit into the story line? Third, decide what problem or obstacle the central character must try to overcome. Fourth, explore the possible solutions to the problem. The characters may be surprised by the solutions needed to solve their problems. Lastly, give your story an ending that demonstrates that the central character or characters have learned something. Following these simple ingredients will result in a story worth telling and performing.

If you do not write your own scripts, finding good material for your group to perform will require at the very least a little bit of legwork sorting through resources. Your local Christian bookstore, publishers' catalogs, the Internet, and public or college/university libraries are a great place to start. You may read a dozen scripts or more before you find one that is appropriate for your group. You may want to appoint a reading committee to cull through the many available scripts to find material that is appropriate for your group to produce and perform.

When you find a script of interest, check to see if the publishing company charges a small fee for the use of the script and if a royalty must be paid per performance. Check near the title page for the name and address of the publishing company (see Appendix 1 for names and addresses of publishers). Usually these fees must be paid regardless of whether you plan to charge for admission or not. It is important to pay these fees so as not to incur an embarrassing lawsuit for your church. These fees are generally very modest.

Musical productions tend to be more expensive and may require a deposit for vocal scores, conductor scores, and orchestration. Often these fees must be paid in advance of receiving the materials from the publishing house. Generally, one must give the publisher the following information: The name, address, and phone number of the producing organization, and the name, address, and phone number of the contact person responsible for the production. The publisher may ask when the performances will take place (always call or write a minimum of 6 to 8 weeks in advance of the first scheduled performance), how many performances are scheduled, the seating capacity of the auditorium used for the performances, and the ticket price. Specify whether tickets are general admission or tiered pricing, which means one price for children under 12, a different adult price, and a reduced price for senior citizens; or if you have a graduated price scale based upon the location of the seating. (That is, seating that has the best view is priced higher than seats in the rear of the auditorium.) Please note that when you give the seating capacity number to the publishing company, you should specify the exact number of seats you plan to *sell*. Let's say you have a 1200 seat auditorium but plan to sell only 500 tickets per performance. It is important to provide this information because the publishing company will otherwise charge you a higher licensing fee. This is true for musicals, where royalty fees are based on the number of seats you will be selling per performance. The licensing fee is then determined by the publishing company. You can be quoted a price either on the phone, or through a written contract you will receive within five to seven business days from the publishing company.

Some publishers include the right to produce a play or scene in the price of the script books; no additional fees are necessary. Other publishers require only one script book purchase and grant your organization the permission to photocopy additional scripts as needed. The latter approaches usually apply to one-act plays or short scenes. The licensing rules vary from one publishing company to another, so be sure to check with your particular publisher for their licensing requirements.

Contacting publishers well in advance of the beginning of your rehearsal period has multiple advantages, not the least of which is providing ample time to receive the needed scripts and related materials. Most publishers have a variety of ways to ship the scripts and scores to you. You may have a UPS or Federal Express option or regular U.S. mail. Be prepared to choose the option that works best for your particular time frame.

Let me add a cautionary note here. Most publishers are very sensitive about placing the most accommodating people in their order rooms to best service the requests of people who may be making first-time orders. Most of the time when I make a call I talk to a friendly customer service person who seems to enjoy talking to people from around the United States. On rare occasions, quite frankly, I encounter representatives who are not as sensitive. I still brace myself every time I make a call to a particular New York publishing house. When I get a less than helpful person on the phone, it always makes me think twice about whether I want to do business with this company again. Admittedly, this rarely happens, but my advice is to try to enjoy the novelty of the situation if someone is rude. It makes for a good story to tell later.

In summary, the drama group should learn from how the church has used drama in the past and use that as a springboard for the future. The recruitment of members for your drama team should be as inclusive as possible. The team should identify its target audience and establish general as well as specific goals they seek to accomplish. The team should always begin early with planning as finding, creating, developing, or selecting dramas to use can be very time consuming.

Division of Leadership Roles

Every group needs a leader. Make sure the leader you choose is someone who is sensitive to the needs of the group, its members, and to the church and community being served; someone who can help arbitrate and maintain the delicate balancing act of keeping people productive and happy; and someone who is willing to commit his or her time to the ongoing challenge of keeping the group focused and active. It is also important, in my opinion, that this person be someone who is generally respected by the entire drama team. Look for a person who is fair-minded, excited by ideas, and a good nurturer and mentor. I think a good leader needs to be approachable, willing to listen to others, and capable of making tough decisions when they have to be made.

It's probable that you are reading this book because you plan to be the group's leader or have already been designated as such. Remember that no one has mastered the qualities I've listed; don't let them intimidate you, but do let them guide you.

As for other leadership positions your group may need for your ongoing drama ministry, I think that decision rests with your group. While some teams may function better with a more formalized organizational structure, others may find this too stifling. I do think it is important to delegate specific responsibilities to individual group members, rather than saddling one person with too many things to do. If you do not delegate, the burnout rate will be very high for your team's leadership. Regardless of how you go about organizing your team's ministry, be open to change and don't be afraid to learn from experience. Your team will be healthier in the long run if some division of responsibilities takes place in your early formative stages. As I indicated earlier in this chapter, leadership will require a significant commitment of time and effort, and given the fact that people are so incredibly busy now, be mindful of fairly divvying up tasks among your group's team members.

Suggestions for Special Meetings

Regardless of where you live, there are more than likely some great resource people within your community. Probably many members within your own congregation have a variety of talents and abilities they can share with your group. The truly remarkable thing about being involved in theater is that it draws on virtually all aspects of daily life. The variety of things that one learns by being involved in producing plays can be a major part of the enjoyment for the church drama group. Producing a play is a tremendous learning experience. Plays are set in different time periods, influencing how they will be interpreted. Researching customs, clothing, or relevant historical events that pertain to the play you are producing is just one way to learn by participating in theatrical projects. Another enrichment experience comes from working with the wide range of the people you may tap as play participants. Meeting and working with new and different people can be one of the most refreshing aspects of involvement in the drama group.

Your group may be comprised of eager beginners who have a burning desire to be involved with a drama group, but have very little knowledge about how live theater really works. This is perfectly okay. Everybody has to begin somewhere! I think it is preferable to admit openly that you do not know everything there is to know about a certain subject. Lifelong learning is pursuing interests and developing those interests in the continued quest for knowledge. Try to create an atmosphere that is open to anybody desiring to be a part of your group. Encourage participation by finding ways to channel a prospective team member's talents into your group.

Early on in your group you should identify a list of resource people in your community. This list may include teachers in the local high school, community college, or university nearest you. Ask someone from the local community theater or professional theater to come and talk to your group, or offer to travel to them. I have found over my professional career that artists generally love to talk to people and share their ideas about performing. After all, this is their business—communicating with other people. Do not be afraid to call and arrange for someone to speak to your group. You may be very surprised to learn that professional actors and artists have many goals that mirror your work in the church.

Learning How to Analyze Performances You See

As a teacher, I routinely require my students to see productions of plays as part of any theater course I offer. I always remind my students before they go to any production that, regardless of their opinion of whether the play is enjoyable or not, hundreds, even thousands of hours have gone into the execution of that production. They must learn to analyze why a production is successful or unsuccessful. I usually require written evaluations by the students, delineating what they liked and what, if anything, they did not like. Then they must address the most difficult question: "Why?" Everyone can have an opinion about theater. We do not necessarily have to know anything about an art form to state an opinion as to whether we like it or not. But when we must explain why, we begin to learn how to analyze what we see. I think it is good for a person to go into any performance desiring to see the best possible work. Our expectations are often lowered or heightened by the reputation of the producing organization, but I always try to go into any production as though it is potentially the best theater I may ever see. Because of that attitude, I have seen remarkable productions at churches, schools, community theaters, and professional companies. I have likewise seen more than my share of plays that did not quite live up to my expectations.

Learn how to constructively critique what you liked about the production. Analyze why you think it may not have worked. Try to be positive in your approach. Ask yourself a series of "why" questions. "Why did I not like the overall interpretation of the play?" "Is my quarrel really with the script?" "Do I disagree with the director's interpretation of the script?" "Why did the music and choreography seem to work in this musical, but the book/dialogue did not work?" or vice versa.

In conjunction with seeing as much live theater as possible, arrange a tour of a facility or request a "talk-back" session with the actors, designers, or director of a production. This is an excellent way to ask the kinds of questions that you are very interested in having answered. A backstage visit or talk-back can usually be arranged with any producing organization as long as the request has been made in a timely fashion. I suggest a minimum lead time of two weeks. This interaction will allow your group an extraordinary insight into the workings of a particular theatrical organization. It can be exciting for your own group to learn how particular problems in a production were creatively solved by the production team. It has been my experience that nearly all producing organizations are obliging of these types of requests. You just need to ask. A tour or talk-back may last 15 minutes to an hour. Just remember the producing organization is doing you a favor, so be respectful of their time. Honor them by being courteous, asking questions, and acknowledging your appreciation at the time of the occasion and through a simple follow-up thank you note. If you follow this advice, you will have a much easier time in the future arranging this type of event for your group.

One note of caution as you consider these types of opportunities for your group: Be sure that someone in your group researches the content of the material being presented. The title or playwright of the script being produced may not be enough. One summer I was working in a professional theater company and a play by Tina Howe entitled *Painting Churches* was being presented. It is a rather innocent sounding title. Many patrons thought that maybe this was something like the film *Lilies of the Field*. Upon watching the play many patrons were very surprised to learn that the play centered on a young artist who decided to do a portrait of her parents, whose last name happened to be Church. The daughter's relationship with her parents and her basic attitude toward them was something many patrons were offended by as they watched the play. So be careful when arranging this kind of event for your team's members. When making ticket reservations, ask the box office personnel for a plot synopsis (or read the play script in advance) and be very aware of your group's comfort zones concerning the material being presented onstage. After all, you want this to be a positive experience for your group. Reading the play beforehand or carefully asking questions of the box office personnel when you inquire about a certain production will prevent any sort of embarrassing situation for your group. Theater can and will often deal with delicate issues in a straightforward manner. It can often make us feel uncomfortable in a variety of ways. It is not necessarily bad to deal with certain delicate issues through dramatic productions; just use common sense in discerning what is appropriate for your group to see. Often seeing other groups perform can serve as a real inspiration for your team members. Many ideas can be gleaned from seeing quality theater productions. I strongly encourage your group to take advantage of the opportunities that may exist in your community to see other productions.

Building a Support System

A good support system consists of a group of people who encourage one another to do their best work. Your drama team can begin to develop a real sense of camaraderie. This is where the edification of one another takes place. Within the context of doing virtually any drama, questions will arise that will have potentially long-lasting effects on those connected with the production. When actors are trying to interpret their lines in such a way so as to sound believable, to ring true to the audience that will be eventually hearing and seeing the production, powerful things can happen. Unbeknownst to you or others participating in a production, the script may be touching the life of a fellow actor in a deeply significant way. This reflection of life is part of the appeal of working on a script. But sometimes the scripted material can hit home a little more closely than anyone could have predicted. Part of what is involved in providing a good support system must include, in my opinion, being sensitive to each other's needs by being comforting, compassionate, and spiritually accountable to the members within your group.

Performing in plays or weekly sketches demands that the actors involved find ways to make their characters believable. Even far-fetched characterizations or "caricatures" need to have something about them that is believable. The most effective actors find ways to identify with the characters they portray. Usually something in a character will be analogous to one of the many roles that each of us plays out daily. In my own life I'm a parent, a teacher, an administrator, a supervisor, a husband, an artist, and a student of life, to name a few. In these various roles I'm sometimes happy, sometimes sad, and sometimes exasperated or frustrated. I have a working context of emotions and responses to certain situations. Even though much of my life involves doing public things in front of an audience, I can still be the shy little boy who forgot his single line in an Easter program when he was five, and then went careening through the aisle of his church at breakneck speed while the entire congregation howled with laughter.

We're all very complex human beings. Acting certain roles in sketches or productions affords an opportunity to therapeutically deal with the broad spectrum of emotions that most humans encounter in their daily living. Whether his ultimate goal is to make an audience member laugh, cry, or think, an actor must find a way to meaningfully and believably engage the audience in his character's development. The better job the actor does in making a character ring true, the more an audience will involve itself in the production. This candid examination of self and self-motivation is one of the most wonderful discoveries an actor can make. Sometimes this realization takes place in just reading a part, or during the rehearsal process, or even during the performance. The powerful impact theater can have on an individual actor, the whole acting ensemble, and the audience can be quite incredible. Be supportive of your team's development in every way possible.

Think carefully about who the best person is to play each role in every sketch or production your group chooses to perform. The insights your actors may gain from playing roles that are very close to their own lives, or the lessons they can learn from playing roles that are very different from their own experience, should always be carefully considered by the team's leadership. Try to keep an open mind and not pigeonhole people into only doing serious roles or comedic ones. The ongoing drama ministry needs to foster and nourish the development of actors who can perform a wide variety of roles. Learn to trust your instincts about assigning roles, but also be prayerful in your consideration of who may gain the most in the long run by having an opportunity to play a specific part. This type of ongoing support and development will enrich the lives of your team's participants in ways you cannot even imagine. I have often been placed in the difficult situation of choosing the right person to perform a certain role. I try to think objectively about what each person might gain from the experience and who will work well within the ensemble of people who will eventually be performing with each other. It's not always easy. Sometimes it is downright painstaking. In the end I must make a decision and not look backward.

My next role as director is to help each person rise to the occasion of performing the roles I've assigned. At that point I invest my energy in finding ways to convey and communicate to them what I need from them and how they can develop their characterizations. Rehearsing, in many ways, is my favorite part of putting a dramatic sketch together or mounting a full-fledged production. In rehearsal, I see actors begin to identify or find ways to use their life's experience in the development of their characterizations.

Lastly, realize your group will grow and change with time. This evolution of the group will involve including newcomers in your team's ministry. As I indicated before, this may be accomplished by incorporating new members into your group at any time, or once or twice a year. Do whatever seems right for your group. But do allow others to join in the fellowship and ministry of your team. As your group evolves, continue to seek ways to keep it challenging for the veterans and to embrace, support, and nurture the newest members of your group. Try to remember how hard it may have been for you to commit yourself to this team's ministry, and the difficulty of time management you personally faced in trying to include this creative work in your busy schedule. Try not to forget your feelings of being easily intimidated when the group first formed. Your sensitivity will make newcomers feel welcome in joining your group. Devote some time and much prayer to the ongoing development of your drama team's ministry to your particular congregation and to the many needs of your community.

While a significant portion of this section of the book has been devoted to supporting and nurturing the performers, please note these same courtesies should be extended to anyone seeking to contribute to your group's success. This includes anyone who may want to provide technical assistance through making costumes, finding props, or building sets, or to those who may enjoy trying their hand at writing and developing sketches for your group to perform. Do not overlook the importance these people will have in your group's development and ongoing ministry. Just take everything one step at a time and remember to be a good encourager.

Training the Actors

*S*ince you are eager to have spiritual gifts,

try to excel in gifts that build up the church.

1 Corinthians 14:12, *NIV*

Chapter 4
Training the Actors

Basic Concepts and Performance Theories

Acting is both the easiest and most difficult thing a person may strive to do. It's easy in the sense that we all learn how to act by imitating others. We learn at a very young age what behavior is acceptable and what is unacceptable in a social setting. We learn through observation of others, most critically those whom we admire the most. Acting, by its very nature, is something learned by doing. A person can be familiar with all the performance theories that exist, only to fail miserably at trying to recreate one believable moment on stage. The great acting teacher and theorist, Sanford Meisner, summed up acting this way: "Acting is living truthfully in imaginary circumstances." This, in my opinion, sums up the craft of acting about as concisely as possible.

The discussion of acting would be incomplete, though, without a mention of the influence of the great Russian theorist, performer, director, and producer, Constantin Stanislavski. The Stanislavski influence on acting style has dominated the way actors have worked for most of the twentieth century. Stanislavski stressed the importance of making the character's life as real as possible. Actors must leave no stone unturned in developing a characterization onstage that is believable to anyone in the audience viewing the performance. One of the secrets to acting, according to Stanislavski, is a series of "magical what if" questions each actor should answer about his character. By delving into these questions, the actor defines, decides, and refines what emotional, physical, and vocal choices are appropriate for any role he or she may play. These choices need to have a logical progression even if the logic is only true for the actor playing a certain character.

While there may be clearly defined goals and objectives that the entire acting company wants to accomplish, how each individual gets there depends on the choices he makes. This is what makes acting a unique, individual expression. The goal of the acting ensemble should be to clearly present the material to the audience. Finding unity in the style of acting is important; otherwise, the impression the audience is left with is that the performers are all doing their own thing. Therefore, the leadership of your drama team should acquaint themselves with a few of the ideas and theories of acting. After trying some exercises from different acting theorists, the group will slowly evolve a working style that best suits its needs.

In my own teaching of acting I borrow from the ideas of a dozen or more acting theorists. I try to take from each of them ideas that I have found successful. However, the method I draw on the most is firmly grounded on the ideas and theories of Stanislavski. My suggestion to your group is to experiment with the games and activities you will find in this book and then expand on these games on your own to suit your group's specific needs. Then, I suggest trying to read some books on the subject of acting.

In teaching others how to act I adopted early on a maxim I try to abide by. This is simply "There are no rights or wrongs to acting and the only rules to effective acting are the ones you discover for yourself." At first this may seem like a cop-out, but further exploration and practical application of this principle will reveal something else. While most people may try to solve a particular onstage problem a certain way, there has to be room for individual expression. As director or teacher your goal should be trying to frame the style of acting in such a way that you achieve a unified look. You need to have a fairly clear idea of how you want the material to be interpreted, make the best casting choices available to you, and then blend the whole performance into something that rings true for the audience. A certain amount of individuality needs to occur in shaping the performance through rehearsals, and it is the responsibility of the director to find ways to unify the actors to get at the heart and soul of the characters being represented, as well as making sure the tone is neither too heavy-handed or too weak. Just remember that actors have ideas, opinions, and solutions to problems that occur onstage. Listen to their suggestions and ideas because we all do not necessarily do the same thing the same way. The freedom to make choices allows the performer to express himself in a unique manner. Experimenting through trial and error eventually leads the actor to the best choices available for any given role. This approach is not only time consuming, it is utterly exhausting. I think if an actor tries to be as believable as possible onstage with the physical action and finds a way to make the words of the script ring true, then he will be successful. The challenge for the director becomes making the performances turned in by all the actors onstage as even and believable as possible. Remember that any good production is only as good as its weakest link. For further information on major acting theorists and resource books on the subject, see Appendix 1.

Involving the Beginning Actor

Everyone has to start some place. No one should feel embarrassed about having never been in a play. I would much rather work with an enthusiastic beginner than someone who thinks he already knows everything. The beginning actor usually needs a lot of encouragement. He needs to be welcomed into the process, and those in charge should always assume they must communicate clearly what they expect to accomplish during rehearsals. What may be common knowledge for some in your group never occur to the beginner. I remember one time when I cast a young woman in a play. She was perfect for the role. However, as I began to block the opening sequence with her at the first rehearsal, I suddenly realized she did not have the foggiest notion of what I meant by upstage, downstage, stage right, or stage left. It didn't take much more for me to know that this very talented and gifted young woman had never been in a play before. So we just took a few minutes to cover some of the basics. The confused look on her face disappeared and she eventually delivered a sterling performance.

The point is that any actor has to begin somewhere. That somewhere may be with your congregation's drama ministry. You will no doubt constantly couple more experienced performers with new actors when preparing dramatic pieces. What I love about beginners is their enthusiasm and energy. The most simple idea may be a marvelous revelation for them. To realize this is to realize one of the sincere joys of teaching and nurturing others. Do not assume anything. Try to make your group one in which new members will be welcomed and greeted with courteous respect for what they bring to your organization. To this end, I developed a "Do's and Don'ts" handout that I give to all new drama participants. I have included a condensed version of this in Appendix 2. Contained in this handout are general terms and ideas for the beginning performers, which will also serve to refresh the memories of the more experienced ones. It can be used as a guideline for what is expected from each team member. Sections can be added or deleted to meet the needs of your group.

The primary reason for having such an instrument in place is to assist new members with understanding what is expected of them and to remind the veteran performers of how your group functions. Too often these things are not done and people have to learn the "rules" by trial and error, which is not a good idea. Also, by having the goals and objectives of your group clearly stated, your group will be better informed and will get more accomplished in the long run. I am reminded of too many instances in my life where everyone assumed everybody else knew how to accomplish a certain objective, only to discover there were only a select few in the know, while everybody else was clueless. So do yourself a favor. Don't assume anything. Clearly stated policies will save everyone involved in your drama ministry a lot of time, and will help to ensure clear communication with all of your members.

Keeping the communication lines open to everyone in the production, especially the newcomer, will help reassure the members of your group that they are being thoroughly informed, and also that their contributions are appreciated.

Common Errors of the Beginning Actor

A beginning actor may have the right look for the part, interpret the lines effectively, but may have no idea how rehearsals work. They may be totally unfamiliar with basic stage terminology (see Chapter 5) or not understand that actors should not sit around chatting while the director is trying to block or rehearse another scene. This presents a potentially formidable challenge to any director. While the problem is not insurmountable, it certainly must be dealt with in as positive a way as possible.

I think having a separate meeting to welcome the new members before they meet with the rest of the group may be the least intimidating way to integrate new members into your drama team. Using this session to let them ask any questions they may have may help them tremendously in the long run. It also allows the person(s) in charge to really get a handle on how much or how little each person knows about acting and performing. Everyone needs to have that first experience. The way your group cultivates, embraces, and enables new members to successfully contribute will only make your group's work better in the future. Some people love to work with beginners; they love to pass along basic information and to teach others the ropes. Seek these people out and place them in a nurturing, mentoring capacity to make new members feel welcomed.

Dealing With the "Seasoned" Actor

A little knowledge can be a dangerous thing. There is sometimes an erroneous perception that once a person has been in one scene, skit, sketch, or play, he has learned and mastered everything he will need to know about all plays. Oddly, I sometimes feel like just the reverse is true. The more I produce plays, the less I feel like I know. In other words, the more I work with performers, the more I discover different ways the material could be presented. I have more options at my disposal and I must decide which ones I will use. There are two basic kinds of seasoned actors: those who feel like they know everything there is to know about playing a scene effectively, and those who feel like they are constantly learning about what makes a line work, how to get the most out of a laugh, or how to make a dramatic line ring true and effective. While you probably will not have to treat the so-called "seasoned " actor with kid gloves, you may find that some people rely on old tricks and bad habits to get them through a performance. Your job as director might be to reenergize and refocus this person's performance. The "seasoned" actor probably poses the greatest threat to the novice director. My advice is that most actors still want the director to do his job. This may require a little give and take, but then, that is true in almost all ventures.

Theater Games and Improvisational Techniques

The following games and activities should provide you with ideas of how to teach drama to others. This is just a sampling and is meant to merely whet the appetite. More theater games and activities can be found in Appendix 3 of this book. The exercises and related activities are ones that I routinely use in teaching acting students, regardless of their age. I have found that virtually all of these exercises, with slight modification, work as well for seven year olds as they do for senior citizen classes in which I have taught students in their eighties.

Acting is doing. In my opinion, the only rules to acting are those discovered by active participation. I also strongly believe there are no right or wrongs in working with these exercises. You are limited only by your imagination. I encourage you to be open-minded as you work through these exercises. If you are going to be leading an acting workshop, you may want to work through the exercises by yourself first, and then try variations of the exercises that are easiest for you to understand and teach others. When you use them, you will very likely discover how exciting it is to help others find the creative beings that reside within them. More importantly, you may discover something new about yourself and how you relate to the world. The exercises and activities are meant to be fun. The games will also help your group to break the ice and make the task of working together less intimidating.

Action Exercises

Each participant should select a simple everyday action to "act out," for example, brushing one's teeth, combing one's hair, fixing a bowl of cereal, feeding the family pet, or heating something in the microwave oven. The participant should then develop a simple sequence of action that has a clearly defined beginning, middle, and end. The sequence does not need to be very long. It may have a dozen steps or so in order to have three clearly defined segments. For this initial exercise, keep it simple and direct. The actor should keep in mind that this is a pantomime. No real objects will be used, but the actor will try to imagine using the object needed to complete the sequence of action. Also, it is my recommendation that no sound or words be used to execute this exercise. This will help the participant to focus solely on the action. Once the sequence of action has been determined, the participant should rehearse the sequence until it is finely tuned. After it has been refined, the actor should move on to the next step.

By this time each actor should have begun to imagine a setting in which this action is taking place. Is he in his bathroom at home, a public rest room, the kitchen, or another setting where one may be trying to complete this task? Fill in the details about the setting. What does the room look like? What color are the walls? Is there a mirror? How big is it? How is the room lit? Is there a window in the room? And so on. Then have the actors focus their attention on the size, shape, weight, and texture of the imaginary objects being used in the exercise. It may be helpful at this point to allow the participants an opportunity to work with the actual objects they have been trying to re-create. They then can move back and forth from the actual object to their re-creation of it as a pantomimed imaginary object. Depending on the age of the participant, you can spend any-where from five to twenty minutes on this exercise.

Brushing Your Teeth

Let's say you have chosen to work through the simple action sequence of brushing one's teeth. This is a good exercise to begin with, because even small children brush their teeth a couple of times a day. For the older participants, it is a simple action they have been doing for years. It poses very little threat to them to simply reenact something they have done since childhood. Perhaps your sequence goes like this: First the person picks up his toothbrush in the hand he normally uses to brush his teeth. Next he picks up a tube of toothpaste. Not a pump style, not a flip cap style, but a tube that has a cap that will need to be removed. He removes the cap from the toothpaste and applies a small amount of toothpaste to the brush. He returns the cap to the tube of toothpaste. He turns the faucet on for a moment to wet the brush and the toothpaste. He turns the faucet off. Then he begins to brush his teeth. At appropriate intervals the participant mimes spitting out the foamy paste, and then completes the exercise by rinsing off the brush, rinsing his mouth by filling a small cup with water from the faucet, turning off the faucet, placing the toothbrush back to its original place, and then perhaps picking up a towel to wipe his mouth. This represents a clearly defined action that likewise has a clearly defined beginning, middle, and end. It may take 30 to 60 seconds to adequately execute the exercise. Once the simple sequence has been mastered, you may try the following variations for fun.

Still with no sound, focus only on action. Work with imaginary objects that are smaller. The toothbrush is teeny, tiny. The tube of toothpaste is small, the cap very small as well. Making all the objects larger. Get more creative. Repeat the sequence, but this time use normal-size objects in a narrow space. Or tiny objects in a short space. Or large objects in a wide space.

The last variation might be to incorporate sound, but not words, into the sequence of action. Encourage the actors to make appropriate sounds for squeezing out the toothpaste from the tube and turning the water on and off. The toothbrush exercise is one I have used for nearly 20 years in teaching students the fundamentals of acting. It is so simple, yet it focuses on nearly all the essential ingredients to good acting: sequence of action, focus, concentration, and believability. We can also add the obstacle or conflict that makes drama work. It is a good lead-in exercise to the one that follows, another pantomime exercise. It is one I call "the library exercise."

In front, to both sides, and behind the actor there are imaginary shelves that contain books of all sizes and shapes. These books may be on the top of the shelf, in the middle of the shelf, or on the bottom of the shelf. Thus, there are three areas of space—high, medium, and low. The participant is asked to choose a book from one of the shelves that surround him from either the top, middle, or bottom of that imaginary shelf. The next step is to open the book and look at the picture, graph, or illustration on that page, look at the second page, turn a page, look at the third page, close the book, return it to the shelf, and begin the process over again, making a new set of choices. Pay particular attention to the size, shape, weight, and texture of each book selected. Then add variables. For example, tell the actor that the library is about to close, providing a new motivation for the actor. Tell the actor that he cannot find the one book he needs, or he's too short to reach the top shelf. Is it a new book? a book that is old and fragile? a musty smelling book? a book that reminds the person of someone, or an event from one's past? Continue to expand on ideas or associations people have with books.

This exercise can be done with many people at the same time. I think it is an interesting experience to watch this exercise unfold by having several participants act out the sequence while others watch. The participants acting out the sequence can add an entrance and exit to the exercise and some other motivating factor, such as that they are running late for something else but have to do this first, or that they hope to see that special person at the library but eventually tire of hanging around to see him or her. Another way to add some fun to this exercise is to have all participants write down on a piece of paper a set of given circumstances to be played out. Set a time limit, probably two to four minutes at most for each scenario. Tell participants to keep in mind that this, as well as any acting exercise, should always have a clearly defined beginning, middle, and end.

This exercise works best initially if all participants onstage are more or less acting in a vacuum. In other words, they are unaware of the other people onstage with them. Therefore, the focus stays on the individual trying to clearly play out his intention for being onstage in the first place.

Variations on a Nursery Rhyme

The following exercise is a group activity and should be fun for all the participants. Divide your group into two or three smaller groups of at least four to five people. You can do the exercises with more people in each group, but as you read the following instructions you will see why I have limited the number. This exercise can also be used to give members of your team an opportunity to direct. The activity could also be guided by one person suggesting the way the story is going to be acted out, leaving the details as to how to do it to the individual groups. Begin with a nursery rhyme. Let's say you are going to use "Jack and Jill." Review the words: "Jack and Jill went up a hill to fetch a pail of water. Jack fell down and broke his crown and Jill came tumbling after." These words become the basis for the script. Then, using the following ideas, try performing the script in a variety of ways. First, suggest that this is a highbrow gathering of literary people. They have gathered to hear a prize-winning author read excerpts from his newly-written literary masterpiece ("Jack and Jill"). The author may be introduced to the assembled audience and then offer an interpretation of the text. Once completed he could answer questions about what motivated him to write this story in the first place.

Next the group might interpret the piece as though it is being done in a foreign language. Or it could be done as a TV news bulletin, complete with an on-the-scene investigation, reenactment, and interviews with those who witnessed the scene. Another interesting device might be to perform the nursery rhyme as a musical comedy, complete with songs and choreography. After improvising the scene three or four ways, have each group choose two or more of the ways they improvised the script and put the ideas together into a sketch they will eventually perform for each other. For example, Jack may be a highbrow writer, Jill may be a foreigner, the whole episode might be broadcast on a TV news bulletin. Or this new musical version of the classic tale of Jack and Jill might be shown on the weekly entertainment portion of late-night television. The results of this activity can be hilarious. End the session with having each group perform for each other. You'll be amazed and delighted at the many variations your group will come up with as they experiment with this familiar story.

After trying out just a few of these exercises, the leader may notice a rather interesting thing happening. When you watch others "act out" things they have either done themselves, or observed others doing a thousand times, you may find that the re-creation seems oddly mechanical, untrue, or unsure. Oftentimes the actors may seem to be afflicted with a kind of paralysis that makes the simple task being acted out look awkward or cumbersome. Likewise, you may be surprised to learn that some of your group members may have enormous potential based purely on the ability to "invent" or create an absolutely amazing sequence of action that is not only unique, but a joy to watch. This is where, as leader, you will begin to be able to see the potential of your group. Remain open-minded, stress the fundamentals before moving on to anything more difficult (remember, the actors may not have spoken a word yet), but be sure pantomimed action is clearly understood before moving on. Look for clarity and specificity in taking actions apart. Keep it fun, though! These exercises may result in intermittent lapses of focus or purpose, but that's okay. Allow your group an opportunity to laugh at each other and to laugh at themselves. These creative activities will have their fair share of foibles and fumbles, but again that is perfectly okay. While the members of the group enjoy themselves, they will also learn a valuable lesson about performing together. They will learn that performing involves a certain amount of risk taking. Sometimes the risks involve laughing at yourself. For additional acting exercises and theater games, see Appendix 3 of this book.

Exit Stage Right, Kill the Lights, and 86 the Bench

*W*ise men store up knowledge.

Proverbs 10:14, *NIV*

CHAPTER 5

Exit Stage Right, Kill the Lights, and 86 the Bench

Basic Stage Terminology for the Not Quite Ready for Off Off Broadway Actor

It is a good idea to have a working knowledge of certain terms and phrases that assist in the communication process of doing live theatrical productions. The theater, like everything else in the world, has its own vocabulary. Any drama group needs to be able to speak the language of the theater and understand what is meant by a certain term or phrase. For instance, the name of this chapter means the actor on stage would leave the stage by going out the entrance that is to his right as he stands onstage facing the audience, and that someone should turn off the lights and remove the bench from the stage. If you hang around the theater long enough, you will learn a lot of unique and colorful phrases. I have provided some basic vocabulary in this chapter that consists of the essential terms to know. Most of the terms provided in this glossary are defined in the context of working on a proscenium-style stage. (If you don't know what a proscenium stage is, look it up!) This will most likely be similar to the main stage of a sanctuary or the front of a fellowship hall or gymnasium stage. I also use the generic term of "actor" to refer to either a male or female performer on stage.

There are nine basic stage areas on a proscenium stage. See grid below.

USR upstage right	USC upstage center	USL upstage left
CSR center stage right	CS center stage	CSL center stage left
DSR downstage right	DS downstage	DSL downstage left

AUDIENCE

The areas closest to the audience are the downstage positions. Those farthest from the audience are the upstage positions.

Stage Directions

Blocking: The term used to describe the physical arrangement of an actor's movement onstage. Also used to refer to the patterns of movement a director will give an actor.

Stage right: The actor's right as he stands onstage facing the audience.

Stage left: The actor's left as he stands onstage facing the audience.

Downstage: Positions that are "down" toward the audience.

Upstage: Positions that are "up" away from the audience.

In: Facing in toward the center of the stage.

Out: Facing out from the center of the stage.

Areas of the Stage

Onstage: The part of the stage visible to the audience.

Backstage: The areas that are behind the scenes or not directly visible to the audience.

Wings: The offstage area to the right or left of the stage; actually a part of the backstage.

Green room: The waiting area for actors, usually used during either the rehearsal or performance of a play. May also be the room where the actors are greeted after a performance.

Body Positions for the Actor

There are eight basic body positions. They are as follows:

Quarter down right: The actor is turned one quarter away from the audience, facing downstage right.

Profile right: The actor stands facing stage right. The audience sees the actor's profile.

Quarter up right: The actor stands with body turned one quarter away from upstage and facing upstage right.

Full back: The actor's back is to the audience. Rarely used, this position can actually become a very strong position onstage. May also be used to give the sense of the actor being closed to the action occurring onstage.

Quarter up left: The actor stands with body turned one quarter away from upstage and facing upstage left.

Profile left: The actor stands facing stage left. The audience sees the actor's profile.

Down left: The actor is turned one quarter from the audience, facing downstage right.

Full front: The actor directly faces the audience.

Open body position: An "open" position is one in which the actor strives to be as open to the audience as possible. In arranging people onstage, one of the most basic problems a director must solve is making sure that the audience can see the actors onstage, especially as they speak and react. There are always exceptions to the basic rules, but generally an actor "shares" a scene by standing in a quarter position. An actor generally tries to gesture or pass objects with the upstage hand and will generally kneel on the down-stage knee.

Sharing a scene: The term used when the actors are both equally open to one another onstage. This allows the audience to see and hear the actors equally.

Upstaging: A derogatory term that means that someone is taking the focus away from what should be the major focal point of a scene and calling attention to himself. This is often referred to as "mugging," "hamming it up," or "stealing a scene." While this type of performing may have its place in broad comedy or farce, it is generally perceived to be distasteful and disrespectful to the other actor(s) onstage.

Stage Movement

Cross: An actor moves from one area of the stage to another area. When marking a script, it is usually abbreviated with an X. For example: XDR means to cross to downstage right.

Counter: An actor adjusts or "counters" the movement of another peformer onstage. This is done by moving in the opposite direction of the other actor. If one actor moves downstage left, the other might cross upstage right. Countering provides interest in the "stage picture," but isn't always necessary.

General notes on stage movement: The actor, as indicated earlier, should always try to stay as "open" to the audience as possible. It is usually much more interesting to see an actor move on a curved line or a diagonal rather than on a straight line. For example, when moving from an upstage to downstage position, the actor should move on the diagonal. Of course, there are always exceptions. The point is that while stage movement should usually appear as natural as it can, to move on straight planes is just not very interesting visually. Thus, moving on a curved line or on the diagonal, especially when working on a proscenium stage, makes for a much more interesting picture for the audience to look at.

Glossary of Stage Terms

Ad lib: Derived form the Latin, "Ad libitim" (at pleasure), the term applies to the lines supplied by the actor wherever they may be required, such as in crowd scenes. Another term directors use is "hubbub," which means essentially the same thing. These lines help make the scene seem more realistic.

Aside: A line which other actors onstage supposedly cannot hear. Oftentimes asides are done while the action "freezes" onstage. This commentary within the context of playing a scene can be a very humorous device.

Auditions: The term used to describe the process by which productions are cast. Auditions can be "cold" (unprepared) readings from the script, a prepared monologue, or in the form of an interview. Sometimes they will be conducted by using improvisational techniques. Also, auditions can be a combination of all of the above. A synonymous term is "tryouts."

Blackout: When the lights onstage go out. Lights can slowly fade to a blackout. Lights can also "bump," or go out quickly to complete darkness in the theater.

Build: The term that describes the process of working toward a climax in the scene. When one uses the term as "build a costume," it means to make a costume from scratch. Also might be used to describe "building" the set.

Callboard: A bulletin board where information is posted that may be of concern to the entire company.

Calling for a line: What an actor does when he needs to be fed a line or prompted during rehearsal. The procedure should be as follows: When the actor forgets his next line, he says "Line." The prompter or stage manager then gives the actor his next line.

Calls: The times when persons associated with the production are "called" to rehearsal. "Calls" are generally posted on the callboard.

Choices: Decisions an actor must make in order to create a role.

Company: The term used to describe anyone associated with a particular production. This includes anyone acting or performing in the production as well as anyone working in a backstage capacity.

Concentration: The ability to focus on what is necessary and to block out what is unnecessary.

Cues: Abbreviated by the letter "Q." Usually the last line of a spoken passage that cues the actor that speaks next. Also, productions have light, sound, and music cues that are marked into the stage manager's script as places where something occurs. A certain line may be used as a "Q," or signal, to turn the lights on or off, or increase or decrease their intensity onstage. If an actor is asked to "pick up cues," the performer should try to deliver his line as soon as possible after hearing the cue line for his next speech. Often referred to as "taking out the dead air." This makes the action of the play brighter, or quicker.

Curtain call: The opportunity for the audience to acknowledge its appreciation for a performance. Actors may be presented individually, paired, or grouped according to onstage time. Or a curtain call can be done as an ensemble. Curtain calls should be rehearsed as carefully as any other aspect of the production. They are an integral part of any production. A cautionary note: Keep the curtain call as tight as possible. Try not to allow it to go on and on and on. Rehearse the timing so actors know when to enter, take their bows, and when to exit.

Cut: To stop the action onstage. Frequently used in rehearsal to let everyone know that the action onstage is to cease. May also be used in the context of removing a line, a prop, a piece of business onstage, as in cut the line, cut (or remove) the prop, or cut that piece of business.

Double casting: When one actor plays more than one role in a production. Could also mean that two people have been cast in the same role. When a role has been double cast in this way, one performer will perform on a specified date(s) and the other actor will perform on another. Frequently done in productions to allow more people to participate. The downside is that it generally means more rehearsal time will be needed and another costume must be pulled, fitted, or made.

Exit: To leave the stage; also, an opening in the setting through which actors may leave the stage.

Fourth wall: The invisible, imagined, or implied wall through which the audience sees the performance.

Front of house: Usually refers to the area where tickets/concessions are sold/purchased.

Given circumstance: "The givens" of any scene are the facts that are known about the scene that is to be performed.

"Hit the lights": Turn on the lights.

Homework: As in "actor's homework." Refers to the work the actor does before the next rehearsal. Usually involves research at some level.

House: The area where the audience sits to watch the performance.

Immediacy: A quality that actors strive for in their work. Ability that an actor has to make the role and action onstage seem believable.

Improvisation: Often shortened to "improv." This term means to spontaneously improvise or create business or lines onstage.

Indicating: A derogatory term referring to an actor doing something onstage that "indicates" an emotion rather than being genuinely truthful and in the moment.

Intention: The actor's reason for performing an onstage action. Interchangeable terms include "actor's strategy" or "actor's plan."

Justification: How the actor rationalizes what he or she will do onstage.

Kill the lights: Turn the lights off onstage or in the house.

Line reading: Directions on how to say a line or how to interpret a line.

Line rehearsal: A rehearsal specifically used to run lines. May also be called a "line thru." The purpose of this type of rehearsal is usually to help actors memorize lines and for technical cue purposes.

Method acting: An acting process invented by Constantin Stanislavski. Highly influential theory of acting that has dominated twentieth century thinking about how actors act. The main emphasis is making an actor's performance onstage as honest and truthful as possible.

Moment to Moment: The actor doing one thing at a time or trying to progress through a play by placing emphasis on playing each moment to its fullest.

Monologue: A speech by an actor either as part of a scene or alone onstage.

Motivation: The actor's reason to do what he does onstage.

Notes: The time, generally after rehearsal, when the director makes his or her comments to the company. May be done orally or through written notes. Usually done in some sort of combination of the two forms. While writing notes for your actors takes longer, it does help this portion of rehearsal to move more quickly. My experience has been that actors zone out during lengthy notes. So I try to write notes in two ways. One is general or company notes; the second is individual notes to/for each actor. I may include suggestions on how to tighten up a piece of business, an idea to try out to help motivate the line, or a piece of business to add to the scene.

Objective: What the character wants to achieve in any given scene or the play as a whole. The latter, in Stanislavski terms, is referred to as the "super objective."

Observation: Paying close attention to the behavior of real people in real situations. Allows an actor to apply what he observes in reality to his acting.

Obstacle: Any obstruction that gets in the way of an actor/character completing his objective onstage.

Overacting: When an actor pushes or exaggerates his acting so that it is unbelievable.

Pace: The tempo of the production. To "pick up the pace" usually means to tighten the time between cues.

Pause: As in a dramatic pause. Stopping momentarily to emphasize something that has just been said or just realized onstage, for the purpose of making an impact on either the character or audience.

Physicalization: Physicalizing your action onstage, or finding the physical qualities of your characterization. The character may walk with a limp or be hard of hearing in the right ear. Make appropriate physical choices to help clearly define a characterization.

Presets: This term refers to anything that is "preset" before the performance begins. A prop may be preset in a specific place, as may a costume, or a piece of scenery. Lights may be preset to establish a mood or atmosphere in the theater prior to the audience entering the house. Responsibility for presets of props and costumes can be divided in a variety of ways. The prop crew can set them and the actors check to make sure the items have been preset, with the stage manager also checking to see that the task has been done. Or actors can be made responsible for placing the props and the crew and stage manager can double check to make sure it has been done. Double checking ensures that the prop or costume piece will be in place for the actor when he needs it during a performance. Emphasize to all company members not to tamper or move anything that has been preset.

Projection: When the actor speaks loudly enough onstage to be heard clearly in any area of the house.

Proscenium
stage: The traditional "picture box" stage in which the audience is directly in front of the stage, which is usually higher than the audience level and curtained.

Rehearsal: The act of practicing material for the purpose of performance. Rehearsal is the preferred term among professionals. To use the term "play practice" is not necessarily inaccurate, but within the profession, this has a derogatory connotation.

Running Crew: Refers to the technical staff that actually "runs" or operates the lights, sound, etc., for a production. May also be referred to as stagehands. While one person may be appointed as the crew chief or captain, the crew is ultimately accountable to the stage manager.

Run-through: An uninterrupted rehearsal of a scene or act of a play. The director usually takes notes during the run-through. The company may then have a work-through of the material to smooth out the rough edges.

Sense memory: When an actor re-creates an experience onstage by employing the use of one of the five senses. For example, if a character is coming home, the actor may remember the smell of the bread his mother baked when he came home from college.

Stage fright: The fear, anxiety, or panic a performer may feel prior to a performance. This is not an unusual feeling even for the most seasoned performer.

Stage manager: Generally thought of as the director's right-hand person. He attends all rehearsals and oftentimes any conferences the director has with designers. He is responsible for running the show during performances, and making sure the show runs as the director intended it to run. During a show's run, the stage manager gives the following time announcements to the company:

House is open, half-hour: All presets for the show have been completed and the audience is now being seated. It is half-hour until places.

Fifteen: Preshow lighting is up, and fifteen minutes until places. At this time the stage manager will collect valuable packets for safekeeping from each performer. The stage manager returns them to the actors at the end of the show in the dressing room.

Company meeting: Can occur sometimes at fifteen or later. The company meeting is a short time for announcements and a time of prayer.

Five minutes: Five minutes until places. All crew members should be at their places at this time as well.

Hold: So many people are lined up to get in that we will be holding the beginning of the show for "X" number of minutes.

Places: Actors in Act I take their places for the beginning of the show.

In all cases when the stage manager gives a call, the proper response is a simple "thank you" from all who hear the call.

Strike: To remove something from the stage. Also used to describe breaking down the set at the end of the last performance of a production. Another way of expressing "to strike something" is to "86" the object.

Subtext: The meanings, motivations, ideas, and feelings that remain unspoken in any text. Commonly called "what's between the lines." In many ways, subtext can be more important than what is actually spoken.

Thrust stage: A stage that "thrusts" out into the audience, so that the audience is seated both in front of and on two sides of the stage. This stage has no curtain.

Type: The term used to describe the categorizing of actors by appearance or in how they are most likely to be cast.

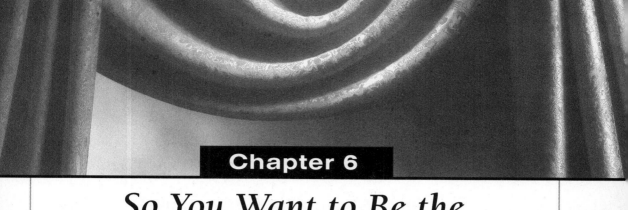

So You Want to Be the Producer/Director?

*J*ust as each of us has one body

with many members, and these members

do not all have the same function,

so in Christ we who are many form one body,

and each member belongs to all the others.

Romans 12:4, 5, NIV

Chapter 6

So You Want to Be the Producer/Director?

The information that follows is given from the perspective of directing a large-scale production. However, while these tips may address things that you will do when directing a big production, I also think you will find yourself applying the information as you prepare weekly, biweekly, or monthly performances for your drama team. Even if your group has already tried doing larger productions, I think you will find information here that will aid you in your endeavors. Perhaps you will discover or rediscover a simple but important principle as you read through the information.

Who's in Charge? Defining the Roles of Producer, Director, and Production Team

You've heard the expression, "Too many chiefs and not enough Indians"? This is an apt way of describing what happens too often when a church (or any other group) decides to produce a play. For better or for worse someone has to be in charge. The person in charge should be someone who possesses leadership capabilities and the ability to generate excitement about a project. He must also understand how to communicate his ideas to other people. He needs to have strong organizational and time management skills. He should also be able to grasp the "big picture" and then all the steps needed to get the production ready to be performed. A very tall order, to say the least.

There are several ways your drama group may decide who will be in charge. For some groups the choice may be obvious. With others it may be a little more difficult question to answer. Either there are many people capable of taking on the responsibility or no one who really thinks he is. In the former situation perhaps it is just a matter of deciding who has the most interest or the most time to commit to the project. In the latter situation the group may need to have a couple of people take on the responsibility of producing and directing the production. While this can lead to confusion about who is really in charge, it is a workable model that I will discuss later in this chapter.

The person in charge will ultimately spend countless hours thinking through the script and solving problems. It is often a thankless job. The person in charge must be willing to take on the responsibility with the understanding he may or may not receive much help from other people. A person who knows how to delegate responsibility and who is not afraid to ask others to pitch in and help will be successful at the job. Consider dividing the roles of producer and director. Within your group there may be a person who is better at scheduling rehearsal space, calling people to remind them of rehearsals, finding people who will help build the set, sew the costumes, hang some lighting instruments, or type the playbill. These are all responsibilities that generally fall into the lap of the producer. While the director may request all these things, the producer will procure the services or items requested to ensure the production stays on schedule. The director directs the actors and works with the assembled production team. The producer's responsibility is to solve all the production needs such as sets, costumes, and lighting. This arrangement can work well with a husband and wife team or two good friends who like to work together. It can work effectively as long as each person does his job. The key to success is that the two people respect one another and try to resolve any differences they may have privately rather than publicly. Even in the best working relationships people are going to have differences of opinion. People who take on leadership positions within any group need to learn how to compromise and be diplomatic with those they are trying to lead.

The bottom line is that producing or directing a production for your church, no matter the size of the production, takes adequate and organized planning. The task is a lot to ask any one person to do, so if the responsibilities can be delegated to two responsible people, so much the better. There are groups that may have an individual who is willing to take on both jobs, to serve as both producer and director of the production. However, it is a highly consuming job. Even the most organized and disciplined person can easily get burned out quickly if he is not careful. So my advice is to break the responsibilities down into the two roles of director and producer. Together they can draw on the strengths of one another to enable the production to live up to all of its potential. The producer will do things such as finding people who will help "produce" the plays: to build the set, sew the costumes, find props, find set pieces, run the lights, run the box office, do the publicity, type up the program, and usher people to their seats. The director then focuses on researching and rehearsing the play with the actors, meeting with the producer and production team as needed, and trying to keep everything on schedule.

As you form your group you will want to take time to clearly define for yourself what it means to take on these leadership roles. Once the roles are defined, all connected with the production will have a better and clearer understanding of what is expected of them. This will go a long way toward helping your group be one that will grow through the experience of working with one another.

Developing a Realistic Strategy

It is perfectly all right to have great dreams and aspirations for your drama group. Always try to be realistic, though, about what your team can and cannot do. In other words, as I've indicated before, take it a step at a time and let your group slowly evolve into what you want it to become. First look at the resources available to you. Some groups may initially be limited by their financial resources in developing an effective drama ministry. Your group may be constrained to just one or two events per year, so take the needed time to carefully plan each venture. After you have tried something, evaluate the success of the experience through the responses you receive from the congregation and also within the group itself. Be true to your overall mission or purpose for doing drama in the first place and decide as a group how best to move on. Again, being realistic will only serve to help your group grow spiritually.

As I stated in Chapter 3, it is imperative that everyone who wants to be in a drama group must understand at the outset the commitment they are making. It must become a priority for those involved in order for the work to be done. A scheduled performance always has a deadline and everyone involved has to be willing to commit to the work in order to reach that goal. It may very well be that some of your team members can and will be able to commit a lot of time and energy to everything you plan to produce. Others may only be able to contribute a little time to each venture or a lot of time to some productions and no time to others. I think it is good to develop a group that can work with this flexible arrangement. If there is plenty of room for give and take, your group will be the better for it.

Analyzing a Script

One of the most basic tasks of a director is to read a script and visualize what it could look like on stage. When I read a script, I do this automatically. But I realize not everyone may. So let me suggest some ways to read, visualize, and analyze a script that may be under consideration for your group.

As you read a script for the first time, make note of the elements that are appropriate for your group. For example, you may want a certain cast size, or you may want a script that will be performed by a mix of ages. So the first step, as we discussed earlier in the book, is finding the appropriate material for your group. As you begin to read a play, what do you "see" in your mind's eye? What do you begin to visualize? The first thing that may come to mind is that the play may be a perfect one to perform in your venue. Or you may decide what at first glance looked like a good play to do is not a good choice because it has too many technical requirements. Try to be open-minded. But do not try to fit a round object into a square hole.

As you read a play the next thing you may try to visualize (beyond the technical requirements of the play) is whether or not you have the people to play the characters. I like to read a play with specific people in mind. Even when I don't start reading a play in this fashion, I usually am reminded of somebody who is just like that character in the play, and then begin to imagine that person saying those lines. It almost always makes me enjoy the play more. You may even find that as you read more and more of the script certain characters will remind you of more than one person you know. This is good because then it is easier to imagine more than one person performing a particular role. The reason I think this is good is that although you may be looking for a particular play to show-case the talent of a very specific actor, what do you do if your group decides to do a particular play, and the person you had in mind to play the lead role doesn't audition? Try to be open to the idea, on a first reading, of any number of people who might be right for a certain role. You may catch yourself laughing out loud as you imagine a particular person saying a specific line or quipping a certain retort. This is good, because then the play is already coming to life in your mind.

Beyond the physical demands of the script, you may also try to visualize what you will need in the area of costumes, hairstyles, and makeup. I think this is important because as you first "visualize" these aspects of a production, you may again decide one script is just too ambitious and demanding but another script is perfect for your group. Learn to visualize a play in this way, by seeing what the characters are wearing and what they look like. Likewise try to visualize whether or not the play needs sound effects or would potentially be enhanced by using particular music. Or maybe the demands of the script are such that cast members need to be able to play musical instruments or perform certain complicated tasks on stage. Ask yourself as you read, "Who in our group can do these tasks?"

Once you have done this you are ready to go on to the next step, which is to decide whether the material is appropriate for your group. This may result in some rather spirited discussion, if the whole group is involved in the process, but in the end your group will need to come to some consensus. You may also want to get the approval of the appropriate member(s) of your church staff. Once the group has made its decision, the next step may be done either by the group, or only the persons who will actually produce and direct the script. The next step has to do with analyzing the play.

I firmly believe the more analysis a director does before rehearsals begin, the more he will have to draw from as the directing process begins. Analysis begins with reading the play several times, perhaps with a different objective each read-through. I like to read a play for analytic purposes many times: once, where I'm focused on just the story and how I may end up telling that story; once, for the purpose of character development; then once each for where to note what is needed in terms of costumes, lighting, set, sound, music, and props, or special effects. I try to make as many notes as possible as ideas occur to me. Keep those notes with you at all times, for as a director, or actor for that matter, you will probably think about this project all of the time. Some of my best ideas may come during the middle of the night or on my commute to and from work. If I have the production book or notebook with me I can jot myself a quick note as it occurs to me, rather than thinking, "Oh, I'll remember that later." My experience has always been that if I don't write it down immediately, I'm going to forget it.

The research portion of analyzing a play is one of my favorite tasks. It can be a pain in the neck at times, but I have found the legwork always pays off. Good research helps a director make up his mind as to why he is making a particular choice. Research previous productions of this particular play. Call another church who did the play and ask their director a few questions. Look at art work, periodicals, magazines, or old photographs, interview people, visit places, look at costume history books, and listen to music from a particular era that might be appropriate for your production. Research can be painstaking, but I think it can be fun. One thing you discover can lead you to the next thing, and so on. All the while, whether you realize it or not, you are subconsciously making decisions about how you will eventually direct a particular production. Try to be as thorough as possible in your research. Where and when appropriate, share much of this information with your acting company, your production team, and running crew. This process does as much as anything to give you confidence as you begin the task of actually "putting the script on its feet."

As important as a good acting ensemble is to the success of any production, its counterpart, the production team, is equally important. The production team is made up of the good people who like to work behind the scenes. Everything that possibly can be done to assure them of their importance should be emphasized early on by the director and producer. I like for the entire company of any production I direct to be as interactive as possible. This helps to foster more of a group camaraderie, rather than an "us" and "them" mind-set between the cast and crew. The latter can be destructive. All of us have different talents, and when these talents are used effectively within a group, each person can feel as though he has made a significant contribution to the overall success of a production. From the beginning your group needs to acknowledge the contributions of everyone who participates at any level. The production team is an extremely vital link to the group's success. In every way possible, try to cultivate an atmosphere that genuinely shows and supports the contributions of everyone whether they are actors or the people who operate the lights.

Selecting a Stage Manager

The stage manager is one of the most pivotal positions in any production. The person selected for this job must be organized, willing to attend every rehearsal, and both a good listener and a person who can demonstrate leadership characteristics. The stage manager is an integral part of the entire production process. On his shoulders lies the formidable task of writing down in some legible shorthand form all the blocking and directions the director gives the actors and compiling all the lists of things needed to execute the production. The person becomes an indispensable assistant to the director. If and when any confusion arises about which actor is supposed to enter or exit, make a cross on stage, or do some particular piece of stage business, the stage manager will assist in setting everybody straight. Through his meticulous noting of blocking and stage business for the actors and the director, he records the way the production is being done. He also writes any technical cues in his master script, usually referred to as the "production book." As the production is performed, the stage manager will call the cues and may assist in setting props during an intermission or before the show begins. Once a production opens, the stage manager runs the show. This allows the director to perform other duties.

The stage manager should be a person who is dependable, reliable, and exhibits initiative and self-sufficiency. Good stage managers are hard to find. Stage management can be an excellent training ground for someone who may want to direct for your group. You may even want to create an assistant stage manager position to further teach the process to newcomers in your group. The stage manager helps facilitate any production in a myriad of ways, so look carefully for the right person for the job.

In summary, finding the right people for the right jobs is a necessary part of bringing your group together for the purposes of producing a play. Be prayerful in your consideration of filling these positions because success will almost always hinge on how effectively these people accomplish their tasks. Try to be realistic in your approach to all matters related to mounting a production. Be very clear about the time and commitment that will be necessary. Work at the process of learning how to visualize, analyze, and research a script for production. Plan everything so you can anticipate and troubleshoot problems that may arise. By all means assemble the most reliable production team you can and treat them all as equal partners. Lastly, search carefully for that person who will perform the duties of stage manager. The stage manager is a vital link to everyone and everything connected to the production.

Casting a Production and Beginning Rehearsals

*B*ut the fruit of the Spirit is love, joy, peace,

patience, kindness, goodness, faithfulness, gentleness

and self-control. Against such things there is no law.

Galatians 5:22, *NIV*

Chapter 7

Casting a Production and Beginning Rehearsals

Holding Auditions and Selecting a Cast

By this point your group has chosen a script to produce and has a director, producer, and production team in place. Now the real fun begins: holding auditions and selecting a cast. There are many different ways your group can hold auditions. Whichever method you use, make sure that the date, time, place, and what is expected of auditionees is clearly communicated to members of your congregation. Do this at least a couple of different ways. Place a notice in your church bulletin or newsletter. Produce a flyer with all the pertinent information and post it in strategic places in your church building. Consider doing a series of special announcements during announcement time in your worship services. By all means, start early, announcing the auditions at least two weeks before they actually will take place. While you still may miss a few people, the majority of those who are interested will probably hear about the auditions.

Once you have decided when and where the auditions will take place, decide who needs to be present to observe the auditions. Include the director, obviously, and perhaps the producer. If the script is a musical, then the music director and accompanist should be present. If the script requires choreography, then the choreographer needs to be there. The stage manager can help facilitate the audition process by handing out audition forms and keeping things moving along. Other than these people and the auditionee, there should be no one else in the room. An extra audience tends to make auditionees nervous, and the audition becomes more like a performance. I do not think that should be your objective during auditions. Try to cultivate an atmosphere in which the person auditioning has the full attention of those in charge. If the person auditioning flubs a line or mispronounces a word, it is not nearly as embarrassing as it might have been if there were fifty other people in the room. I do think it is a good idea for there to be at least one other person in the room with the director and the auditionee at all times. This should be good common sense, but in the excitement of getting the ball rolling, this seemingly minor detail may be over-looked.

My suggestion is that the director have a minimum of two afternoons or nights when the auditions will take place. The auditionees should sign up for specific times to audition. Even if the production is a musical, you probably will not need much more than ten to fifteen minutes per person. Set aside another time for callbacks. This is when you "call back" people that you want to see again. For this part of the process, I think it is all right to have everyone you really think you need to see again in the room. This will give you the opportunity to try certain pairings and hear people read a scene together, which can be enormously helpful in making final decisions about casting.

Next, plan the format you will use and decide what you really need to see and hear in the auditions. Most beginners will be rather intimidated by a prepared audition, which is when the actor does a monologue he has memorized. The monologue seeks to show the actor in his best light. It may show comedic or dramatic abilities or it may show something of the actor's range. Professional actors generally have a repertoire of six or more monologues they can do at the drop of a hat. While you may have a person or two in your congregation who could do a commendable job in preparing something on his own, my advice is to use a format that is far less threatening. Other formats could include cold readings from the script or an interview process. I will describe these and give some suggestions on how you might use these techniques.

A cold reading is when someone is handed a script, given a few directions on what is happening in the scene being read, and then asked to read the role you have chosen for him to read. The term "cold" is used because the presumption is the auditionee has never read the script. This may or may not be true. However, even if someone has played a specific role before and you are having him read the part for you, chances are your sense of how the part will be interpreted in the production you are directing may be quite different from the actor's.

The interview process may begin with the director introducing himself and then asking the auditionee to tell something about himself. The interview process may also include a cold reading. The director may use an improvisational technique such as asking the auditionee to tell a story of something humorous that happened to him. I sometimes use this improvisation in the following way: I ask the auditionees to tell a story in two minutes or less that they either enjoy telling about themselves or a story that their family generally likes to tell about them. I am continually fascinated how such a simple question can unleash a flurry of creative thought. The auditionees usually relax, know immediately the story they want to tell, and have a very clear sense of telling the story with a defined beginning, middle, and end. Add to this a sense of animated energy and you have probably seen some very fine acting.

The next thing I do is to hear anything they have prepared. For a musical the auditionees may have prepared songs to sing. They may have a prepared monologue. If not, I will do cold readings with specific directions to see if they are capable of infusing some of the energy they may have displayed in telling their stories to me through the interpretation of the script. Once completed I try to decide if I need to hear anything else and if not, I thank them for coming by, and tell them what the next step in the process will be. This could be telling them I still have many people to see and that callbacks may be needed before final decisions are made. Or I may just let them know when they will be notified as to whether or not they will be offered a role in the production. In either case, I try to communicate clearly what the next step will be and try not to mislead the auditionee.

As director, be extremely sensitive to the feelings of the auditionee. Even though the person may not be right for the production you are presently casting, he may be perfect for something you have planned later in the year. So try not to alienate anyone. Make everyone feel good about having taken a chance by auditioning in the first place.

After you have seen all the auditionees, the arduous task of making your preliminary casting decisions begins. Some decisions will be very easy. Others may be painfully difficult. Bathe your decisions in prayer. Take your time and make the decision about whether you want to use callbacks to see people again. If you do decide to use callbacks, give yourself a very specific time allotment to see auditionees and accomplish what you need to do. I suggest not letting the callbacks go longer than ninety minutes. I most often limit myself to one hour, although your time frame may depend on how many people you need to see and how many different pairings you want to try. You will discover that you like certain combinations better than others. This may have an impact on final casting decisions. Try to weigh all factors, not the least of which is carefully checking your potential cast's previous commitments or availability for rehearsals. Again, you may need to be creative in scheduling your rehearsals to accommodate everyone you want to cast. By carefully considering all of the factors before you announce your cast list, you will save yourself some worry later on.

Once the cast has been selected, they need to be notified and told when and where the first rehearsal will take place. This can be done by either telephoning the people involved or by posting the information in a place that has been previously announced to the auditionees.

Making Rehearsals Effective

During the first called rehearsal, make any introductions that need to be made and take care of preliminary business. Begin with a short devotion and prayer before moving on to the business of rehearsal. You may need to double check everybody's name, address, and phone number so the stage manager can make a company roster. The company roster will have the actor's names, crew and production team names, and the names of the director and producer. The roster will also have phone numbers where people can be reached during the day or the evening. I suggest the roster be done in alphabetical order, to make it easier for everyone, and a space left at the bottom to add additional names and telephone numbers. I like to get the roster to the company as soon as possible, by the second or third rehearsal.

The first meeting may also be a time to take costume measurements (chart provided in Appendix 4) and for the person doing the set to talk about how your sanctuary, auditorium, or fellowship hall will be transformed into a space to perform a play. After these preliminary items have been satisfactorily achieved, hand out scripts and have a first read through with the acting ensemble. This is usually a delightful experience. Listen and observe carefully how your cast members interact with one another and the enjoyment they derive from hearing the script read aloud. Take note of what is naturally funny or sections that have a nice dramatic feel even in the first read through. I suggest the read through be done without interruption. Time the read through. Chances are the actual playing time of the script will be very close to the time it takes to read through the material. Establish goals you want to accomplish with each rehearsal and try to achieve as much as possible within the time frame you have allotted for a rehearsal.

As you are planning your rehearsals, it is very important to make constructive use of your time. Decide before you get to the rehearsal hall how you are going to stage a certain scene. This will enable you to be more successful with each rehearsal. Sometimes what you initially conceived as the perfect solution to a certain problem you are encountering may just not work. Do not be afraid to ask your actors to offer suggestions, but only if you really are prepared to accept their solutions. Remember, as director you are trying to think and solve problems for the entire production. Actors think in terms of how they individually contribute to the production, so they may have helpful ideas in solving a particular onstage sequence. Try as earnestly as possible to use your time constructively. Call the actors you need only when you think you will need them. There is no need to have people sitting around waiting if they do not need to be there. This respect of time will be greatly appreciated by your actors during the early part of the rehearsal process. The day will come all too quickly when everyone associated with the production will need to be present for extended periods of time. Using time constructively will help all involved feel better about how their time is being used.

Tips for Keeping Things on Track

The key to staying on track is staying focused and being organized. As director you will expend a remarkable amount of time and energy on the task of remaining focused. This requires discipline. As I stated before, once you get started, keep pen and paper available at all times. You never know when another thing that needs to be done will cross your mind. Remember to jot it down immediately.

I suppose the best advice I can give you is to try to remain calm and use your good common sense to get through the experience of being a director. Try not to take on everything. Delegate as much as you can, and use the talents of as many different people as possible. Accept the fact that while it may seem to be easier to do something yourself, it will be better in the long run to share some of the responsibility. Admittedly, this is easier said than done. But do try to let others assist you in the process where and when possible. The pressure of getting everything done and meeting the deadlines can and will consume you if you let it. So learn how to pace yourself, solve problems along the way, and do the best job you can. Try not to let the pressure and frustration level mount to the point you feel like you are going to explode; that is just wasted energy. If the tension gets too high, take a few moments to reevaluate why you are doing this production in the first place. Keep the focus on honoring, glorifying, and praising God through this experience. That will help you keep a sense of perspective.

In summary, try to make the audition experience as enjoyable as possible for everyone. Be pleasant and courteous to everyone who musters up enough courage to audition for a role. Decide on an audition format that will work best for your group. Use a callback time if you need it before making those final casting decisions, and then trust your own judgment. Do not second-guess yourself after you make the final decisions; this will only undermine your capacity to focus and concentrate on the production. Plan rehearsals that are meaningful and use time constructively. Always strive to keep rehearsals on track and to keep everyone as happy as possible during the entire process. Rely on good common sense when push comes to shove and remember to delegate responsibility as much as possible.

Working on a Shoestring Budget

*B*etter a little with the fear of the Lord

than great wealth with turmoil.

Proverbs 15:16, *NIV*

Chapter 8

Working on a Shoestring Budget

Tips for Staying Within Your Budget

Every production, no matter how large or small, needs to have a budget for expenditures. As you begin your drama group, you may have some initial start-up costs to facilitate your work. Work as a team to identify how much financial support you may need from the church, and keep your mind open to ways you may raise your own money if the church's budget cannot accommodate your full monetary request. It is possible that some of the money needed to begin a drama ministry might be pooled from the budgets of other ministries within your church. For example, your group might partner with the fellowship committee to perform a dinner theater for your congregation, or you might team up with the outreach committee to work on a special project. Again, be creative in the ways you integrate your drama ministry into the ongoing life of your particular congregation.

Mounting virtually any production takes some money. However, if you are resourceful, you may discover you can do a quality production on a shoestring budget. This normally requires quite a bit of creative thinking, planning, and problem solving. While this task is shared among the director, actors, and production team, the primary person responsible for keeping the show on budget is the producer. The job can be ominous, but matched with the right person, a great deal may be accomplished with very little expenditure. The producer must be resourceful. He needs to know how and where to find things, how to find the best price, and how to excite others about volunteering their time and services to your production. It is essential that your group find just the right person to fulfill this function for each production.

Try to find someone who works well with people, has a good sense of humor, can be a creative problem solver and troubleshooter, and can meet a deadline. As I indicated in Chapter 7, the producer also needs to be a person who can communicate effectively with the director. There should be lots of give and take. Compromise will need to take place at some point, so these two people must be able to work together.

As your group begins work on a production, the producer and director will need to have a good idea of how much money is available for the project. Make an effort early on to identify people within the congregation or the community who can assist the production financially. Costs need to be investigated and estimated to determine and approximate the needed budget. Try to be realistic. Give yourself a little room for unexpected costs, but once a budget has been determined, do your very best to live within its scope. Staying within your budget will require you to streamline costs, but more than likely shortfalls will be offset by unexpected donations of money or services. For every producing organization I know of, be it church, community, educational, or professional theater, the ultimate goal is to have the final tally come in under budget. This is responsible stewardship and should be what your group routinely tries to accomplish.

Admittedly, the demands of incorporating a weekly performance into the worship service and doing larger-scale productions are two very different issues. While larger-scale work will involve more people and probably need more financial support, a beginning drama ministry of any type will have some expenses. All of these expenses (purchase of scripts, props, etc.) need to be factored into the decisions and plans of your drama team. While ongoing drama on a smaller scale is simpler, it might not elicit the immediate excitement (and financial support) that a "splashy" production does. Often a larger-scale production will provide the impetus for an ongoing ministry by exciting people about the power and scope of drama.

The rest of this chapter addresses various aspects of production, such as costuming, lighting, and sound. Choosing people who are creative and frugal to oversee each area will help you stay within your budget. Be sure to refer them to the resource books in Appendix 1.

Costuming

With each of the subsequent production areas it will be helpful if one person takes on the responsibilities of ensuring the work is being done in a timely fashion. This may or may not be a luxury your group will have initially, but the producer should try to delegate these responsibilities to others as much as possible.

The technical area that generates the most discussion is usually the costuming for the production. Everyone associated with the production will have an opinion about the clothing. There are many reasons for this, the most obvious being that most actors have an opinion about what they look best in, what styles best suit their body type, and what colors they prefer. The person delegated to oversee the costuming for a production needs to be aware of this and try to incorporate some of the actors' suggestions as decisions are being made. The actors, however, need to understand from the outset that they will not be allowed to be too demanding. This must be a collaborative and cooperative process among the costume designer/collector, the director, and the actors. Again, a little give and take is in order.

The costume designer works very closely with the director and producer. The costume designer is responsible for making all decisions about the clothing in a particular production. These decisions involve general concepts and imagery, as well as specifics such as buttons, jewelry, and hair clips. The director needs to stay informed about what decisions are being made. First the costume designer should begin making decisions about what each actor will wear in the production. The costume designer should make a list of what each actor needs, which the designer will use to start finding or constructing the costume pieces that are needed. The designer should compile a master costume plot that can later be used by the costume running crew to check the costume pieces in and out. Find a space within the church to store and hang the costumes. This will help ensure that items remain in one central location. I would discourage allowing actors to take their costumes home with them. Invariably something will be forgotten at home, and on a performance night there may not be time to go home and retrieve the item.

As with every other aspect of the production, a certain amount of organization is necessary along the way. There will still be a lot of last-minute details, but learning to pace yourself will go a long way in resolving problems that will arise.

Scenery and Lighting

Often these two production aspects work together. Once you have decided where the play will be performed, the person in charge of scenery and lighting should begin planning how to convert the space into one that will serve the play's needs. If, for example, the production is to be performed in the church's sanctuary, considerable discussion needs to take place between your production team and the church's minister and support staff to decide when the set can be built. Effective planning may require many meetings. Look closely at the church's calendar and resolve any schedule conflicts as soon as possible. Also, be ready to deal with problems as they arise.

Besides creating an environment that serves the play, the scenic designer needs to be aware of any disruptions that building the set may create, particularly during the week before the production opens. This juggling act will require a lot of effort, but if the church as a whole is supportive of the drama team the congregation will probably enjoy watching the transformation of the auditorium. The crew working on the set should be very sensitive about returning things to their proper places and to plan work sessions around scheduled rehearsal time.

In making decisions about the scenery and lighting, the central questions you should ask are: How will these elements enhance the action that is taking place onstage? Will platforms need to be built to allow the actors to be slightly elevated so everyone in the audience can see the action onstage? How does the lighting enhance the mood or create the atmosphere? Does the lighting serve the purpose of illuminating the actors' faces and bodies? Answering these questions and solving these problems early on will make things run more smoothly during the final days before the production opens. Keep set and lighting simple and purposeful.

Props

The job of property master is for your congregation's best scavenger hunter, someone who actually derives pleasure from finding the needle in the haystack. The task of finding props, or "properties," can be fun, but takes time. Props can be things borrowed from people within the congregation, or purchased. The property master or mistress should pick up things that are borrowed, treat the items with great care, and return the items to the lender as soon as possible after the production closes. This will make it a lot easier to borrow items in the future.

Sometimes props cannot be found, bought, or borrowed. In this case, the prop person either constructs the prop or arranges for the prop to be built especially for the production. The prop person is usually in charge of budget expenditures on perishable goods (usually foods) used in the production. The property master or mistress must purchase the goods, pick up the goods or have them delivered, and prepare the goods (foods) for the performance. Often some of these duties may be delegated to an assistant.

Makeup

A good makeup artist may be needed to help create certain special effects such as aging the actor playing a certain role, or helping someone appear a little younger than he may actually be. The makeup artist may also be in charge of working with the cast's hairstyles, working with wigs, and applying beards and mustaches. There is usually someone within the congregation who can take on these important tasks. While the job doesn't become labor intensive until close to the opening of the production, some planning needs to take place to make sure there are adequate supplies. During the dress rehearsals your cast will have to figure out how much time it takes them to do their hair, apply their makeup, and get into costume. This will vary from person to person, but a good estimate is between sixty to ninety minutes before the curtain rises. It is usually a good idea to have the person in charge of makeup present for the dress rehearsals and at least the first performance to ensure things go smoothly.

Music and Sound Effects

Music and sound, much like lighting, help to create a proper mood and atmosphere for the production. Appropriate choices in this area can go a long way in solidifying certain moments on stage. Music and sound effects can be accomplished in various ways. The sound designer is in charge of this aspect of the production. He finds all the music and sound for a production, while the sound operator runs the equipment during the performance of the production.

The person or persons in charge of music and sound may also be responsible for microphones. Rely on microphones for the actors only as a last resort. Actors should be taught how to project their voices early on in the rehearsal process to eliminate the need for microphones. However, some auditoriums are acoustically "dead," and sound simply doesn't carry, so you may need to use lapel or area microphones. It seems best to delegate this responsibility to your music and sound technician.

Programs

If your group decides to print a program for your production, someone needs to take on the responsibility of putting it together. The person responsible for gathering the information and doing the layout needs to pay attention to correct spelling, good grammar and punctuation, and getting all the appropriate names in the program. This job can only be completed a day or so before the production opens. I usually like to do a "mock-up" a week or so in advance and take it to rehearsal one night to give as many people as possible an opportunity to proof it. I usually supply a red ink pen for people to make corrections. Once the program has been corrected, I try to let a few additional people proof it again before doing the final draft. Before it is copied, I proof it again to make sure everything is correct. Proofing the program will save you the embarrassment of misspelling someone's name or unintentionally omitting certain people. If additional information comes up after the program is printed, an insert can be placed inside, if needed, or an announcement can be made during the curtain speech.

I encourage your group to always include in your program a note concerning taking photographs. Regardless of whether a person taking the photographs during a performance is using a flash or not, taking pictures during the performance disrupts everyone's concentration. By planning a photo call for the production you can help ensure that people can get a record of the event. A photo call is a designated time when photographs can be staged with the actors. The photographs can then be taken in closer proximity to the actors, more clearly revealing their emotions in a specific moment of the play.

You may find it helpful to enlist the help of members of your congregation to assist in the distribution of programs before each performance. The personal touch of being politely greeted by someone as you enter the performance is a great way to begin the evening.

Photographs

When the production is said and done, your group will most likely want some tangible memory of the experience. Plan to provide this in a variety of ways. First, set one block of time aside either at the last dress rehearsal or after one of the performances to stage a few select photographs. Perhaps a talented photographer within your congregation can help. I suggest you initially compile a list of potential photographs. You should make sure that everyone is in at least one photograph. I always like to stage a company shot that includes everyone involved in the production. (This becomes a precious keepsake as the years pass.) Then stage a few photographs from the production. This type of photograph tends to work best when three or fewer people are in the picture. Have the photographer take two or three shots of each pose to ensure that he has a workable shot. Once you have gotten all the staged shots you want, allow the actors the opportunity to have individual shots taken of them in their favorite moments of the show. Being time conscious as I am, I suggest you have a predetermined amount of time to do the photo call. Limit yourself to one hour or less, and abide by your time allotment. Otherwise the photo call can drag on and on.

You may decide you want to have someone videotape your production. This can be an exciting way to remember all of your work on a particular project. My advice is to set up a separate rehearsal for this purpose. While it is obviously easier to videotape the production during an actual performance, the equipment that is needed invariably either gets in the way, or the person operating the equipment has to set up so far behind the audience that the sound cannot be recorded effectively. By devoting a special run-through to this purpose, the video operator can set up closer to the action and will probably get a better video recording as a result.

Finally, begin a scrapbook for your group. Include copies of the program, photographs, clippings from your local newspaper, and your bulletin or church newsletter. As years pass this will become a marvelous legacy and record for your church. Find a secure place to keep these archival treasures, updating the scrapbook with each subsequent production.

In summary, establish a budget for each production, and try to live within the budget. Select one of your best people to perform the role of producer and then assist this person in every way possible. Choose enthusiastic people to help with costumes, lights, makeup, music, and sound. Refer them to the resource lists at the back of this book. With each play your group produces, keep a record through photographs, videotape, and a scrapbook.

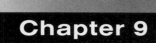

Last Minute Details: Lists, Lists, and More Lists

*C*ommit to the Lord whatever you do,

and your plans will succeed.

Proverbs 16:3, *NIV*

CHAPTER 9

Last Minute Details: Lists, Lists, and More Lists

As director or producer, no matter how diligently you work, there will still be a gazillion things to do during the final week before a production opens. This is where all your planning pays off. However, you may feel so tired that you begin to forget things, so force yourself to keep a list of everything. Write things down as they occur to you or you will forget about them until it is too late.

You must resign yourself to the fact that some things just cannot be done until the last minute. You may not be able to complete the finishing touches on the set until after mid-week services. Costumes you have rented may not be available to you until two days before the production opens. You must learn to pace yourself and believe that things will work out. If you begin to feel stressed, find some time for meditation and prayer to remind yourself why you're doing this in the first place.

As the days pass, remember that you will eventually check everything off your list. You may feel a little numb, yet relieved that your portion of the work is done. The last few days before opening a production will more than likely be a time of real growth for your group. As director or producer you will be called upon to encourage, to reassure, and to nurture your company. Try to be as positive and constructive as you possibly can with everyone involved in the production.

Publicizing the Event

While doing a dramatic production at your church may be primarily for your own congregation, it is a good idea to let others in the community know what you are doing. Theater can be a very effective outreach tool to your community, and it provides a perfect opportunity to invite unchurched friends and family to an event where they can be welcomed into the life of a caring congregation. Make other local churches aware of your upcoming production, and send an article to the local newspaper or request that the paper send a photographer to take a picture of your cast. These are easy ways to get the message to the public. Most local radio or television stations have a community bulletin board or public service announcement that can help promote your event. Be prayerful in your decisions regarding publicity, trust your judgment, and do what is best for your church and your group.

The Curtain Speech

Miraculously, everything is done and the show is ready to begin. If you use a curtain speech to welcome your audience and to make any last-minute announcements, be cordial, brief, and concise. A few days before a production, I begin working on my curtain speech. I try out a few versions of it on my way to and from work. Many times I will write it out so as to eliminate anything unnecessary, seeking to say everything as concisely as possible. Audiences appreciate this effort. Commit the speech to memory, or compile brief notes on a card to which you can easily refer. After welcoming the audience, make your announcements, and get on to the main event. You may want to work on a tag line you'll use for every production. It may take a few productions to discover what's right for you, but try different phrases until you find one that is appropriate for you, and before long you will have your "signature" phrase.

Now What Do I Do?

The best thing for the director to do after the curtain speech is to take a seat in the audience. This choice demonstrates to your company that you trust them to get everything done properly. It sends a strong message to your company that you believe they are capable of doing their particular jobs. Quite frankly, it is nice to collapse in a seat or pew and watch the production. If your group plans to do several performances of the production, you may want to step out in the foyer after the curtain speech. Choose what is best for you and your group. Your group may be comforted by the fact you are watching every performance, or they may need to see you standing in the back of the auditorium. Be sensitive about this, and make the best choice accordingly.

Keeping Your Sense of Humor

By this point you may be asking, "How do I keep my sense of humor?" It's really a tough thing to do. If you are like most people, you wonder how you can invest so much time and energy into something without taking it all too seriously. My response is to take it seriously, but to enjoy yourself along the way. Try not to make mountains out of mole hills, and plan ahead, but take it a day at a time. When the production is finally over, you will be amazed at how much time you suddenly seem to have! Two stories come to mind in this regard; one when I was performing and one when I was directing. About twenty-five years ago I was involved in a touring production of *Godspell*. The director had booked the show in a variety of venues including churches, community centers, hospitals, and prisons. While performing the production at a certain prison site, we were asked that we remain sequestered in a safe, secure space before the show began and during the intermission—a reasonable request. The first act went beautifully.

Everyone, including the prison's staff, seemed to enjoy the show. During intermission we were taken back to our secure room. The door was locked behind us and we all relaxed, trying to catch our breath for the second act. Ten minutes passed, and another ten minutes, until the intermission had been a full thirty minutes. Finally, a guard came to our room, unlocked the door, and informed everyone not to be alarmed, but that during the first act two prisoners had escaped. The guard said the warden needed some time to do a security check before a decision would be made about whether or not we would be allowed to complete the performance. The check was made in the next thirty minutes, and they decided we would be allowed to finish the show. It was a potentially dangerous situation, but our company chose to view it as a truly unique experience.

Once while directing a production of Shakespeare's *Romeo and Juliet* I had another experience where the choice was either to become extremely irritated and mad, or to express my disappointment but try to keep my sense of humor. We had invited a high school group to come for a special late morning matinee of the production. We knew we had a tight time constraint, but thought we could manage to get through the show. Well, the group arrived late. Precious time was eaten away. I suggested we not take an intermission. No, I was told, we had to take a break. Okay, I said, but it can be only five minutes. I was assured that would be fine. We got through the first half in record time, without really sacrificing anything in the performance. The five minute break lasted twenty minutes. I knew we had a serious problem. My actors valiantly tried to race through the second half. Exactly two minutes before the show was to be over, the bus drivers stormed into the auditorium and ordered the students to leave now or be stuck on our campus for another three hours. The students filed out, the actors kept performing, and all I could do was shake my head and laugh. I had never experienced anything quite like that before, nor do I hope to ever experience it again. My actors didn't know what to think. I told them we could either become furious or laugh. We decided to laugh. Believe me, it was the best choice. Being involved in dramatic productions forces a person to be a good manager of time and disciplined in getting things done. So, enjoy the ride, and don't forget how to laugh at yourself.

Chapter 10

Taking the Show on the Road

*W*e are therefore Christ's ambassadors,

as though God were making his appeal through us.

2 Corinthians 5:20, NIV

Taking the Show on the Road

Outreach Potential

One of the goals of your drama group may be to develop an outreach team. There are so many possibilities for this type of work. Touring with drama is rich in mission possibilities, and may just be right for your group. Drama can be an outstanding way to share the message of Jesus with other people. As with everything else we have discussed in this book, the group needs to do some planning before implementing such a program. Focus on the group's strengths and target audience. Your group can then begin to set some goals for achieving the touring objectives.

How to Prepare for Touring

There are so many opportunities for outreach. Your group may decide to perform for children in the community, or for the elderly, or for the handicapped. You may choose to minister to prisoners through drama, or to hold workshops or performances for other churches. There are many service organizations who would welcome your creative output. In our community, the local hospital has instituted an "Arts in Medicine" project. The project seeks to connect artists of all kinds with hospital patients. One of my classes has recently begun visiting the pediatric wing of our local hospital to read books to children. While some of the students seemed a bit reluctant at first, they now routinely volunteer time outside of class to go to the hospital to visit and read to children. No matter how rough a student's day or week may be, visiting a sick child seems to help put things into perspective. Volunteering your services in this way usually requires some kind of hospital volunteer orientation, but it is a wonderful way for your group to serve the community. In our case, I have worked with the volunteer services coordinator and the hospital foundation to purchase an age-appropriate book that the students give to each child during the visit. Whatever your group decides to do, it will be honored by God in significant ways.

If you are contemplating touring, one of the first problems you have to solve is transportation. All of us have done enough caravan-style driving to know it's best to travel in one vehicle whenever possible. If your church has a bus or a van, this is the best way to take a show on the road. If your production will not fit into a van or trailer, then you may have to rent a truck to haul everything. My advice is to keep props, sets, and costumes to a minimum and to travel in one vehicle.

Taking a show anywhere, whether it is just a few blocks or a hundred miles, requires some specific planning. You may decide to plan from the beginning to make your production mobile enough to travel. If this is the case, make production decisions based on how much space you'll have on the van or bus for set pieces, costumes, and props, along with ample room for your actors. The key word is minimal. What's the most minimal way to take a production on the road? Through years of touring, I've discovered that as long as the actors have very basic sets, costumes, and props, performances are effective. When packing the van, try to figure out the best way to get everything and everyone in the vehicle. This may involve taking an afternoon to solve the problem before your first road trip. Have someone write everything down so you'll be able to remember what goes in first and where it goes. After you've done it a few times, you'll probably be able to do it from memory, but having a list ready at all times doesn't hurt.

The person doing the booking for your group will need to develop a list of things to ask the host of the event. A few questions might be: What are the directions to the facility? How long will it take us to get there? What's the best door to enter through? How many people will attend the event? For what age group are we performing? How much performance space will we have? Is there an electrical outlet close to the performance space? Where are the nearest rest rooms? When do we need to arrive? How much time will we have to set up? When will the program begin? What time will it end? These are just a few examples of things you need to ask. Other decisions such as departure time from your church and loading time will be determined by the answers to these questions.

What? You Want Me to Direct Another Production?

*I*n his heart a man plans his course,

but the Lord determines his steps.

Proverbs 16:9, *NIV*

What? You Want Me to Direct Another Production?

Planning Your Next Venture

About the last thing a director wants to think about at the conclusion of a production is, "What's next?" While the thought might cross the director's mind, it may be coupled with the thought, "I will never do this again." Your group may have more than one person who can direct plays; if so, that's great. How can you get started on the next production when everyone is exhausted? The solution is to give yourself a break. Take some time to evaluate the production you've just completed. Return everything that needs to be returned, clean up your mess, and get some rest. Take care of these details at the close of your show, and you'll have a clear head and will be ready to start planning the next project. I would discourage you from having too many productions or activities overlapping one another. People do have lives and need some time to take care of other things. Give your group a respite between finishing one production and beginning to plan another one. Chances are the whole group will be energized by this approach. Remember that when your group decides, plans, mounts, and executes a production, they will have spent hundreds of hours corporately and individually thinking about and working on the production. Other things in their lives have been put on hold. Giving people a break will be the most responsible decision for your group.

With each production or project your group works on, you will begin to have new ideas of what might be best for your group to do next. You may discover that doing the production in the sanctuary didn't work out very well and that next time you want to try the fellowship hall. You may discover you needed more time to work on the costumes, the set, or the lighting. Making note of this information saves you from reinventing the wheel every time you mount a production. Trial and error can be a good teacher. Remind yourself that some lessons are best learned the first time. Be open to new ideas or new approaches. Look for ways to improve your efficiency. Continue to evaluate and determine the priorities of your team's ministry. Decide where your time and energy are best focused, which may mean choosing between large-scale productions and weekly involvement in the worship service. You may, in the infancy of your team's ministry, reevaluate your goals, objectives, and central purpose many times. This is healthy for everybody involved. Your concerns should center on the decisions about how your group can most effectively minister to the specific needs of your congregation. Be candid and honest, but constructive in these evaluations. Use the time in a positive manner, and resist the temptation to complain or bicker. My experience has taught me that very little good comes from complaining.

Consider planning a retreat for your group at the end of each major production to review what worked and what did not. Even if the "retreat" lasts four hours and is in the church's fellowship hall, the carved-out time will allow your leaders to focus and critique.

Another way to give everyone a feeling of closure at the end of a production is to plan a cast party. Cast parties can occur either immediately after the strike of the final performance (make sure the cast knows they are all expected to help with strike) or sometime after the final performance. This is not a time to critique, but a time to celebrate. Look at photographs or the video of the performance. Read aloud any favorable reviews or letters you've received. Have the cast and crew sign each other's programs. The members of the company have probably formed new friendships and may be deeply stirred by the end of the intense rehearsal and performance process. The cast party can be cathartic for everyone.

When planning your next venture, be sure to get the opinions of people you respect regarding the direction you should take. Their objectivity and wisdom can be invaluable. Prayerfully consider such factors as ministry potential, the suggestions of trusted advisors, and the leading of the Holy Spirit in planning the future of your group.

Keep Up the Good Work!

Therefore, since we are surrounded

by such a great cloud of witnesses,

let us throw off everything

that hinders and the sin that so easily entangles,

and let us run with perseverance the race

marked out for us.

Hebrews 12:1, *NIV*

CHAPTER 12
Keep Up the Good Work!

Keeping Your Group Growing and Alive

As with most endeavors, once the initial excitement has worn off, there needs to be a time of reflection and assessment. This will no doubt be true for your drama group. By integrating dramatic experiences into your worship services gradually, your group will have time to grow both in numbers and in spiritual depth. Be open to new ideas your group members may have, and evaluate what your congregation tells you they would like to see. To keep your group growing, investigate other ways it can serve the congregation or the community. After a few successful ventures at church, your group may be ready to consider the outreach potential within your local area. This is an exciting way to grow the ministry. Your group may be ready to invite a guest director to come and work with your team. This infusion of new blood and new ideas can help team members feel rejuvenated and reinvigorated. Conduct a series of workshops designed to teach others the fundamentals of acting or technical theater. Perhaps your group may finally be ready to tackle writing an original drama to be performed at your church. There will come a time when you will need to discuss what's next and where God seems to be leading the group. God will honor your request in ways you have not been able to imagine. By keeping your group vitalized and energized, you will accomplish great things within your own church and in the community.

Making God the Focus

Doing a production that requires so much time, energy, and commitment from a large segment of your church membership should serve as a reminder of what initially brings us together. Our belief in God, and his Son, Jesus, is the unifying force of any work in the church. Dramatic productions can heighten our awareness of what our faith means to us, and can significantly impact our lives. Portraying a character from the Bible, or depicting the events surrounding the birth, life, ministry, death, and resurrection of Jesus can help us begin to truly understand that Christ was a living, breathing human being. One of my favorite professors in graduate school used to describe this as "finding the 'humanness' in characters that we portray." The impact that depicting biblical events through drama has on the Christian actor is important because our understanding and comprehension of Jesus' life on earth is heightened and magnified. As you work with your group and as you cultivate new members for your group, always strive to make God the focus of your work.

Troubleshooting Tips for the Personality Differences That Will Arise

As your group grows both in its scope and size, it may begin to experience a few growing pains. What should the group do next? Some members may be content with doing a few seasonal events; some may want to expand so that productions occur more frequently. Depending on the size of your congregation, your group may be able to do several things at once. More likely though, some tough decisions will have to be made about what your group's next step will be.

The arts tend to attract people with strong opinions. Problems develop when your group begins to grow and certain members want to do one thing while others want to do something entirely different. Probably each faction can make a good case for its idea. There may be no easy solution. Rather than bickering over differences, try to resolve the issue as diplomatically as possible. To this end, it may be helpful to ask a respected elder or your minister to be included in discussions about where your group should be heading.

In all the excitement of being a part of a dynamic team, don't lose sight of your purpose and mission. Foster a sense of mutual cooperation, respect, and flexibility. Learn how to compromise on issues that may arise. It may not always be easy, but try not to let the group dissolve because of power or control issues. Let your group evolve slowly and enjoy the journey together one step at a time.

Constructively Evaluating the Process and Growing as a Team

By doing a single production at your church your group will discover many things about what works and what doesn't work. You'll learn from trial and error. Some people will surprise you, in either a positive or negative way, and you will begin to find out how you work together as a team. Mounting a production has to be a team effort. One or two people cannot do everything and remain happy doing it. Devise a way to constructively evaluate your group's efforts after each venture. This can be accomplished in many ways. It's best to do this evaluation as soon as possible after a production closes, while it's fresh in everyone's minds, and everyone knows what was great and what was terrible about working on the production. It's a brave group that can do this successfully as soon as the production is over, but it's the best way.

A second possibility is to give everybody a break for a week or two, perhaps asking each person to write down one strength and one weakness of the production for your discussion later. This method will tend to get at the heart of what needs to be fixed and what seems to really work for your group. A third possibility is to have the director, producer, stage manager, and production crew leaders get together and evaluate the production, and then have a separate meeting with the acting company. The task takes time, but I think it is worthwhile. Try not to let the session turn into a complaint-fest. Keep the meeting positive and constructive. Build on your strengths and learn from your mistakes. Keep your sense of humor, throw in a dash of common sense and respect for others, and your evaluation session can and will be productive.

Building Up New Leaders

One of the delightful dividends of working on a production is that certain people will demonstrate characteristics of initiative, leadership, and responsibility that may be harnessed for your group's potential growth. Continually nurture new people to assist at all levels of producing a play at your church. Grooming new people for positions of leadership can contribute in other ways to the group's development. The last thing any group wants to do is to "burn out" its members or leaders, so be on the lookout for people who have talents for leading others, and try to find safe ways for them to test their abilities. Don't spring too much too soon on anyone. Be patient and allow people to develop a step at a time.

In summary, allow your group to grow and to try new things, all the while keeping in tune with the congregation. Diligently keep God the focus of your group, and be diplomatic in resolving differences among your group's membership. Learn how to constructively evaluate each production experience. While emphasis should be placed on your group's positive strengths, try to be aware and receptive to your weaknesses and areas where you can grow. Continually nurture new leaders within your group to allow the drama ministry within your congregation to grow in the future.

Appendix 1

Resources

Addresses of Publishers

Many of these publishers will send you a complete catalog upon your written request. I would suggest using your church letterhead. Some of these companies sell scripts outright, others require royalties, and others may rent scripts and scores to you. Please note that these names, addresses, and telephone numbers are subject to change.

Anchorage Press
Box 8067

New Orleans, LA 70182

504-283-8868

Music Theater International
421 West 54th Street

New York, NY 10019

212-541-4684

Baker's Plays
100 Chauncy Street

Boston, MA 02111

www.bakersplays.com

Pioneer Drama Service
PO Box 4267

Englewood, CO 80155-4267

303-779-4035

Contemporary Drama Service

Box 7710-T9

Colorado Springs, CO 80933

800-037-5297

Rodgers & Hammerstein Theater Library

229 West 29th Street, 11th Floor

New York, NY 10001

The Drama Bookshop

723 Seventh Avenue, 2nd Floor

New York, NY 10019

212-944-0595

Samuel French, Inc.

45 West 25th Street

New York, NY 10036

212-206-8990

Dramatist's Play Service

440 Park Avenue South

New York, NY 10016

212-683-8960

Standard Publishing

8121 Hamilton Ave

Cincinnati, OH 45231

800-543-1301

Heinemann Educational Books

361 Hanover

Portsmouth, NH 03801

603-778-0534

Tams-Witmark Music Library

560 Lexington Avenue

New York, NY 10022

800-221-7196

Lilenas Drama

Nazarene Publishing

2823 Troost Ave

Kansas City, MO 64141

816-931-1900

Word Publishing

3319 W. End Ave, Suite 200

Nashville, TN 37203

615-385-9673

Zondervan Publishing

5300 Patterson SE

Grand Rapids, MI 49512

800-876-7335

Friendship Press

PO Box 37844

Cincinnati, OH 45237

800-889-5733

FaithQuest

Brethren Press

1451 Dundee Ave

Elgin, IL 60120

800-441-3712

Abingdon Press

201 8th Ave. S.

Nashville, TN 37202

800-251-3320

Judson Press

PO Box 851

Valley Forge, PA 19482

800-331-1053

Web Sites for Scripts

Here are some wonderful web sites for information regarding scripts and dramatic sketches for worship services. While the Internet is a great source for information, remember that web sites do change periodically and without notice. The listing provided is by no means an exhaustive list; it is given as a way to get you started in your search. It is another resource tool to use, and with the ongoing development of technology is most certainly going to be a fixture in the way we gather and disseminate information in the future.

http://www.curtcloninger.com
Curt Cloninger's web page. You may purchase his scripts online at this site.

http://www.lifelines.ndirect.co.uk./christina
Christian Plays From South Africa by Christina Perrelli. May be downloaded for free. She asks that in exchange you contribute to the missions ministry of your choice.

http://www.micharon.demon.co.uk/MENU.html
A Censored Christmas. A 90 minute Christian musical (or pantomime) written specifically as a means of spreading the Christian message over the Christmas period.

http://members.aol.com/crtsjames/home.htm
Common Belief Drama & Productions. The drama and production part of Common Belief Ministries assists churches and organizations in production matters. All scripts, music, and assistance are free.

http://www.metrocast.com/JohnnyV/Drama.html

Free from the Mega Package. Samples from the "Mega Package of Youth Dramas" package. You may print out the drama and use it as an aid in your local youth ministry or drama department.

http://www.znet.com/~haynese/ewh/

Eric Haynes' Drama Consortium. You can download a multimedia version of all his plays. You must have an IBM PC.

http://www.cs.bham.ac.uk/~pjm/art/dramatic/scripts/

Scripts at the Drama Corner in Pete's Lair. Set of scripts from Peter Marshall in the UK.

http://home.earthlink.net/~revralph96/

Reverend Ralph and Company. Series of comic sketches by several different writers.

http://members.aol.com/cmtoday/clowning.htm

Clowning Around. Great variety of clowning supplies and resources from Randolph J. Christensen.

http://www.dramashare.org/

Drama Share. Maintained by John and Hudy Alexander from the central Canadian city of Saskatoon. Drama Share provides a full-service site for church drama ministry workers. Visit the site to get scripts, staging suggestions, even the sound files necessary to perform the script. Also contains an updated list of drama publishers and writers.

http://www.softray.com/

SoftRay Resources drama library. A database of over 2200 dramas from the major drama providers: Willow Creek, Third Floor Drama, Plastow, Lillenas, Woed, Church Street Press, Pillar, Slice O' Life, and more. You can find dramas by topic, Scripture, author, publisher.

http://www.prostar.com/web/rjlee/drama.htm

Anastasis Theater. Has links to other Christian drama sites, sites with scripts you can download and individual plays and sketches by Robert J. Lee.

http://www.lundboox.demon.co.uk/books/T225.html

Religious Drama, Lund Books. Scripts available.

http://homepages.enterprise.net/trevor/drama.html

Greyfriars Drama. Original scripts from around the world.

http://www.micharon.demon.co.uk/index.html

The Incredibly Useful Christian Music and Drama Page. High quality material for holidays, sketches, or new songs for your worship team.

The following theatrical supply sources may help solve those problems associated with mounting a theatrical production. From renting costumes to finding opening night gifts, this list should prevent you from having too many sleepless nights. I suggest phoning for a catalog.

American Fencers Supply Company

1180 Fulsome Ave

San Fransisco, CA 94103

415-863-7911

Looking for fencing equipment, foils, swords? This is one of the best sources in the United States.

NORCOSTCO, Inc.

Atlanta Costume

2089 Monroe Drive NE

Atlanta, GA 30324-4891

404-874-7511

Fax: 404-873-3524

Also a complete line of makeup, lighting instruments, gels, gobos, etc.

Baum's Costume and Accessory Catalog

Dance and Recital Apparel

106 S. 11th Street

Philadelphia, PA 19107

1-800-8-DANCIN (832-6246)

Broadway Costumes, Inc.

954 West Washington Blvd., 4th floor

Chicago, IL 60607

1-800-397-3316

Also a complete line of makeup supplies.

The Music Stand

1-802-295-7044

Need an opening night gift? Have your credit card number ready.

Milliner's Supply Company

911 Elm Street

Dallas, TX 75202

1-800-627-4337

Need a hat? Trim for a wedding dress? Call now.

Gamble Music

312 S. Wabash Ave.

Chicago, IL 60604

1-800-621-4290

All of those hard to find musical instruments.

LMI of Itasca, IL

1776 W. Armitage Ct

Addison, IL 60101

1-800-456-2334

So you don't find what you need at Gamble. Call LMI.

Acting and Production Resource Books

The following books may be great resources for your group as you develop your team. These are all excellent sources of information to further your understanding of theater. (Many may be out of print but are probably in your local library.)

Acting

Adler, Stella. 1988. *The Technique of Acting*. New York: Bantam Books.

Berry, Cicely. 1973. *Voice and the Actor*. New York: Macmillan Publishing Company.

Blunt, Jerry. 1967. *Stage Dialects*. New York: Harper and Row.

Boleslavsky, Richard. 1987. *Acting: The First Six Lessons*. New York: Theater Art Books.

Brestoff, Richard. 1995. *The Great Acting Teachers and Their Methods*. Lyme, NH: Smith and Krauss.

Chekhov, Michael. 1953. *To the Actor: On the Technique of Acting*. New York: Harper and Row.

Cohen, Robert. 1984. *Acting One*. Mountain View, CA: Mayfield Publishing Company.

—. 1998. *Acting Professionally*. Mountain View, CA: Mayfield Publishing Company. Fifth edition.

Cole, Toby. 1970. *Actors on Acting*. New York: Crown Publishing.

Delgado, Ramon. 1986. *Acting with Both Sides of Your Brain*. New York: Holt, Rinehart, and Winston.

Fox, Meme. 1987. *Teaching Drama to Young Children*. Exeter, NH: Heinemann Educational Books.

Hagen, Uta. 1973. *Respect for Acting*. New York: MacMillan Publishing

Company.

— .1991. *A Challenge for the Actor.* New York: Scribner.

Harrop, John and Sabin R. Epstein. 1990. *Acting with Style.* New Jersey: Prentice Hall.

Hobbs, William. 1973.*Stage Combat.* New York: MacMillan Publishing Company.

Johnson, Neil K. 1990. *The Drama Sourcebook of Principles and Activities.* Highland, UT: Stage Door Press.

Lewis, Robert. 1980. *Advice to the Players.* New York: Harper and Row.

Linklater, Kristin. 1976. *Freeing the Natural Voice.* New York: Drama Book Specialists.

—. 1992. *Freeing Shakespeare's Voice.* New York: Theater Communications Group.

Machlin, Evangeline. 1988. *Speech for the Stage.* New York: Theater Arts Books.

Mayer, Lyle. 1991. *Fundamentals of Voice and Diction.* Dubuque, IA: Wm. C. Brown Publishers.

Moore, Sonia. 1984. *The Stanislavski System.* New York: Penguin Books.

Perry, John. 1997. *Encyclopedia of Acting Techniques.* Cincinnati: Betterway Books.

Spolin, Viola. 1963. *Improvisation for the Theater.* Evanston, IL: Northwestern University Press.

Stanislavski, Constantin. 1936. *An Actor Prepares.* New York: Theater Arts Books.

— .1949. *Building a Character.* New York: Theater Arts Books.

— .1961. *Creating a Role.* New York: Theater Arts Books.

Whelan, Jeremy. 1996. *New School Acting.* West Collingswood, NJ: Peacock Productions.

Costumes

Boucher, Francois. 1967. *20,000 Years of Fashion.* New York: Harry N. Abrams.

Cunningham, Rebecca. 1989. *The Magic Garment: Principles of Costume Design.* White Plains, NY: Longman.

Dryden, Deborah. 1982. *Fabric Painting and Dyeing for the Theater.* New York: Drama Book Publishers.

Ghorsline, Douglas. 1952. *What People Wore.* New York: Viking Press.

Ingham, Rosemary and Liz Covey. 1980. *The Costume Designer's Handbook: A Complete Guide for Amateur and Professional Costume Designers.* Englewood Cliffs, NJ: Prentice-Hall.

Kafka, Francis. 1959. *The Hand Decoration of Fabrics, Batik, Stenciling, Silk Screen, Block Printing, Tie Dying.* New York: Dover.

Reader's Digest. 1976. *Complete Guide to Sewing.* Pleasantville, NY: The Reader's Digest Association.

Russell, Douglas. 1973. *Stage Costume Design: Theory, Techniques, and Style.*

—.1980. *Period Style for the Theater.* Boston: Allyn and Bacon. Englewood Cliffs, NJ: Prentice-Hall.

Vogue. 1981. *The Vogue Sewing Book.* New York: Vogue Patterns.

Props

James, Thurston. 1987. *The Theater Props Handbook.* Cincinnati, OH: Betterway Books.

Motley. 1975. *Theater Props.* New York: Drama Book Specialists.

Stage Makeup

Buchman, Herman. 1974. *Stage Makeup*. New York: Watson-Guptill Publications.

Corey, Irene. 1968. *The Mask of Reality*. New Orleans: Anchorage Press.

—. 1990. *The Face Is a Canvas*. New Orleans: Anchorage Press.

Corson, Richard. 1989. *Stage Makeup*. Englewood, NJ: Prentice-Hall.

Frank, Vivien and Jaffe, Deborah. 1992. *Making Masks*. Secaucus, NJ: Chartwell Books.

James, Thurston. 1990. *The Prop Builder's Mask-Making Handbook*. Crozet, VA: Betterway Publications.

Scenery and Lighting

Arnold, Richard. 1994. *Scene Technology*. Englewood, NJ: Prentice-Hall.

Asix, Vern. 1956. *Theater Stagecraft*. Anchorage, KY: Children's Theater Press.

Barber, Phillip. 1928. *The Stage Technician's Handbook*. New Haven, CT: Whitlock's Book Store.

Carter, Paul. 1988. *Backstage Handbook*. New York: Broadway Press.

Cunningham, Glen. 1993. *Stage Lighting Revealed*. Cincinnati: Betterway Books.

Fitzkee, Dariel. 1931. *Professional Scenery Construction*. San Francisco: Banner.

Friedrich, Willard J., and John H. Fraser. 1950. *Scenery Design for the Amateur Stage*. New York: The MacMillan Company.

Gillette, A.S. 1960. *Stage Scenery*. New York: Harper and Row.

Parker, W. Oren and Harvey K. Smith. 1974. *Scene Design and Stage Lighting*. New York: Holt, Rinehart, and Winston.

Walters, Graham. 1997 *Stage Lighting Step by Step*. Cincinnati: Betterway Books.

Stage Direction

Cohen, Robert and John Harrop. 1984. *Creative Play Direction.* Englewood, NJ: Prentice-Hall Inc.

Dean, Alexander and Lawrence Carra. 1989. *Fundamentals of Play Direction.* New York: Holt, Rinehart, and Winston.

Shapiro, Mel. 1998. *The Director's Companion.* Orlando: Harcourt Brace College Publishers.

Web Sites for Traveling Drama Ministry Groups

The following lists sites of groups who tour throughout the United States and present opportunities for Christian performers.

http://ww4.choice.net/~dcooksey/
Friends of the Groom Drama Group. More than just theater, the Friends of the Groom (FOG) specializes in entertaining audiences and challenging them with the Christian message at the same time. Also provides training workshops.

http://members.tripod.com/~Lords Players/LP.html
The Lord's Players. The Gospel like you've never seen it. College group that travels around the state of Georgia.

http://mcia.com/~calstan/index.html
Network Drama Team. Twelve teenagers and one adult bringing the gospel through drama.

http://www.teleport.com/nonprofit/tapestry/

Tapestry Theater Co. Located in Portland, Oregon, and serving the Great Northwest. They are glorifying God through the dramatic arts.

http://www.newlife.org.n/drama.html

New Life Drama Co. in Concord, MA, who do all their productions to glorify God.

http://www.cita.org/

CITA (Christians in Theater Arts). The home page for a non-profit organization dedicated to the service of Christians involved in theater and related arts.

http://www.geocities.com/Broadway/2371/high/

The Official Common Ground Website. High energy music and drama ministry that goes on tour every June.

http://www.horizongate.org/

Horizongate. A ministry of theater and video production based in San Diego, CA.

http://www.open.org/~cnmip/

Master's Image Productions. Dedicated to communicating the gospel through dramatic arts.

http://www.nldc.com/

New Life Drama Company. They are a full-time traveling drama ministry. They travel 350 days out of the year to the churches, schools, prisons, nursing homes, and the streets.

http://www.rain.org~cpchuckt/

Covenant Players. Thirty-two year old ministry with 120 teams. Use their web site to contact them for booking purposes.

Some Do's and Don'ts for Participants in Productions

Some Do's and Don'ts for Participants in Productions

Your group may want to devise a handout that describes some basic do's and don'ts for drama participants, which includes procedures your group follows. I used to go over this information aloud at the first rehearsal. I finally decided it worked better (and was less time consuming) to print a handbook for people participating in our productions. Feel free to use it as written or to modify it as your group deems appropriate. Most of the information is very basic, but actors and technicians find it extremely useful in preparing for rehearsals. You do have permission to photocopy any portion of this section for your group's purposes.

INTRODUCTION

As a drama ministry group we aspire to regard anyone associated with our productions with the same decorum, respect, and etiquette that is expected in the professional theater. It is expected that everyone affiliated with our productions abide by the following rules.

Everyone associated with our productions is to be treated with respect. Common courtesy is expected from every actor and every technician connected with our productions.

The following guidelines cover rehearsal musts, performance necessities, and other pertinent information. Please know that these tidbits of advice come from years of experience in the theater. In order for our productions to operate smoothly, this information must be read with utmost diligence.

I.   REHEARSAL MUSTS

Check the callboard for call times. Be on time or preferably a few minutes early.

Always bring a PENCIL to rehearsal, along with your assigned script. Do not use an ink pen to mark your script. Often the director may change the blocking he or she initially gave you.

As the director begins blocking a scene, refrain from talking unless you have a specific question about the blocking. If the director is blocking a scene with lots of actors on stage at once, resist the temptation to talk to others. Even whispering can be very distracting and annoying. Remember while you as an actor may be concerned only about where you move at a given moment in the script, the director is trying to think and imagine what everyone onstage is doing at the same time. Directing requires an enormous amount of concentration.

During rehearsals try to learn your lines, cues, and pieces of business as quickly as possible. Try to memorize the lines quickly so you can begin to work "off script." If you go blank on a line during rehearsals, call for "line," and the prompter or stage manager will give you the line. If you forget a line at a high emotional point, it is perfectly all right to call for the line with the same emotional intensity you may be performing at the moment. This will help you stay in touch with your feelings for that given moment in the script.

You may find it helpful during rehearsals to wear shoes that are similar to the ones you will be wearing in the production. Likewise you may find it helpful during rehearsals to wear clothing similar to the clothing you will eventually wear onstage. For example, if your character wears a jacket, sweater, or hat, it may be helpful to rehearse with that item, even if it is not the actual item you will wear. This will allow you to practice pieces of business that you will do onstage. This will also make the technical rehearsals, in regard to dealing with costumes, go much smoother.

Be a problem solver during technical rehearsals. Please don't create problems. This means listening to the expert (director, designer, or crew person in charge) about how best to execute a quick costume change or accomplish a hasty property exchange that needs to take place offstage. Technical rehearsals are used to solve these problems. Don't panic, just be alert and logically help solve the problem.

II. PERFORMANCE NECESSITIES

As soon as you arrive at the theater each evening, sign in. The sign-up sheet is on the bulletin board in the green room.

Actors should always check their own props and will almost always do their own Act I presets during dress rehearsals and performances. All actors must clear the house by half-hour (term meaning half-hour before performance begins), therefore all costume, props, and set presets must be done by this time.

Likewise, all crew members must have assigned tasks completed by half-hour, such as cleaning the house, placing signs, checking sound, and warming up lights.

Company members are encouraged to use the designated rest room facilities prior to performance and during intermission times.

It is the company member's responsibility to perform as directed. No pranks on fellow company members will be tolerated or permitted. Failure to abide by this rule could result in you being replaced. It is all right to have fun with the performance, but not in ways which interfere or detract from it.

After the performance, actors should get out of costumes (and hang everything properly) before greeting visitors.

The stage manager will give the following time announcements to the company during dress rehearsals and performances:

House is open, half hour: All presets for the show have been completed and the audience is now being seated. There is a half hour until places.

Fifteen: Pre-show lighting is up; fifteen minutes until places. At this time the stage manager will collect valuable packets for safekeeping from each performer. The stage manager will return them to the actors at the end of the show in the dressing room.

Company Meeting: Can occur sometimes at fifteen minutes or later. The company meeting is a short time for announcements and prayer. Actors who appear at the top of the show are expected to be in makeup and costume by the company meeting.

Five Minutes: Five minutes until places. All crew members should be at their places at this time as well.

Hold: So many people are lined up to get in that we will be holding the beginning of the show for "X" number of minutes.

Places: Actors in Act I take their places for the beginning of the show.

In all cases when the stage manager gives a call, the proper response is a simple "thank you" from all who hear the call.

Actors and technicians usually establish a routine during the run of the production. Respect the fact that some people like to be alone to concentrate on their performance. Some people like to joke around, listen to music (this is okay, but bring headphones), or talk. Everyone prepares differently. Use common sense to prepare for the evening's performance. Focus on "the world of the play" from half-hour to curtain. Some people may feel like they need more time than the director schedules for them in order to complete their hair, makeup, or other assigned duties. It is usually all right to arrive a few minutes earlier than called. However, never arrive later than call time.

Actors are expected to arrive in ample time to the place where they will be making their entrance.

When waiting in the green room area, keep the door shut to the hallway, the overhead light off, and remain quiet.

III. OTHER PERTINENT INFORMATION

Whenever the director or set designer schedules a work call, all company members shall be in attendance for the duration of the call. Attendance will be monitored through the use of a sign-in sheet.

Only with express permission from director may any changes be made to an actor's appearance. An actor's appearance at the time of audition was considered when casting (hair style, hair color, facial hair). Trims or alterations to appearance will be the responsibility of hair and makeup design. It is not the actor's responsibility or even within the actor's freedom to alter his or her appearance without first discussing this with the designer or director.

Props are generally placed on the prop table areas in the green room or stage. Please do not move or play with the props and always return props to the prop table after they have been used on stage. Actors are personally responsible for these items.

Since our theater does not have reserved seating we operate under a first-come, first-served policy for seating. Taping off of seats for special guests will not be permitted. The box office opens at one hour before performance time and the doors open thirty minutes prior to the performance.

No one should enter the booth area except those personnel assigned to be there. Technicians are not permitted to have food or drinks in the booth. Likewise, actors are personally responsible for any costumes and makeup used. Put costumes and makeup away in their designated places when finished.

Treat costumes with the same respect that you would your own finest clothing. Eating, drinking, and smoking in costumes is strictly forbidden. It is the actor's responsibility to properly hang all costumes and return them to their appropriate place on the rack at the end of each rehearsal and performance. Failure to do so will result in one warning being issued, followed by a fine of $10.00 per offense.

The stage manager has many duties during the course of any production. The stage manager is in charge of the show from the opening night performance until closing. This individual is the troubleshooter for any problems that may arise during a performance. If an assistant stage manager is designated, he should be accorded the same respect and attention as the stage manager.

For many actors and technicians, being in a production is about waiting. Use time constructively. For example, you may have a scene and then a seventy-five minute wait for curtain call. Bring reading, sewing, or quiet games to occupy the time.

CONCLUSION

Do every performance as though it is the last one you'll ever give to an audience. Focus on the world of the play and totally commit yourself to your character and what you discovered during the rehearsal process. Always commit your performance to the glory of God. For technicians, my advice is the same.

Directors strive to be good managers of time. But we do have deadlines. In order to meet these deadlines, actors and technicians need to be dependable and responsible. When running a show, always pay meticulous attention to the fact that you are contributing to the success of the overall production. For instance, a technician should time a sound cue or light cue with a feeling for the action that is taking place on stage. Realize that assisting an actor with a quick costume change is an important part of the play. Regardless of your task, concentrating on the play will ensure that we all will function much more effectively. Keeping your sense of humor in productions is a necessity as well, regardless of how stressful the deadlines get. The team effort is the key. Working together for a common cause will unite us in a very special way for years to come. In the end, doing your best work is about your own personal integrity as a human being, your own discipline, and your own work ethic. Art is almost always about striving for perfection. God deserves nothing less than our very best effort.

Acting Exercises

Experiment with these activities and tailor them to your group. Have fun!

Observation Exercise

This is a wonderful exercise to use with the beginner. The purpose is to motivate the participant to develop his capacity for seeing and observing other people. The exercise is really quite simple. Ask the actors to observe someone performing an ordinary task which has a very well-defined beginning, middle, and end. After observing this activity, ask them to rehearse a reenactment of what they saw. Have them prepare this and then show it to the rest of the group at the next session. The participants should not tell the people they are observing that they are doing so. The people being observed would likely modify their approaches to performing even the most mundane tasks if they knew someone was watching. Encourage actors to watch from afar. This will allow them to scrutinize much less obtrusively. Give group members some examples of behaviors to observe, such as making a pizza, washing windows, cleaning up a mess in the mall food court, or putting on makeup. I usually do not give many examples to my students because I find that when I do, they tend to do something I have given as an example. If actors do not discover their own activities to observe, one of the primary objectives of this exercise is lost. The actors need to become increasingly aware of their surroundings and the human beings they encounter. Learning how to observe others is also enormously beneficial to directors. A director can learn a great deal by observation. Such observation may help the director explain a certain scene or spark inspiration for a piece of stage business he may want to include in his production.

Variations

Mimic the actions of someone everybody in your group knows, either a famous person or someone in your community. This type of physical impersonation might be fun for your group.

On individual scraps of paper, write down several characterizations that an actor may attempt to recreate. Use extreme descriptions to get your actors warmed up. An example of an extreme characterization is a thousand year old man trying to bend over to pick up something he dropped on the ground during a snowstorm. Have each actor improvise actions related to the characterization he draws from a hat.

Completing a Task

This exercise involves two people working together. Limit final performance time to two to four minutes.

This is a good follow-up exercise to either the action exercise (toothbrush), the library exercise, or the observation exercise. Divide your group into pairs. Designate one person from each pair to think of a simple sequence of action that has a beginning, middle, and end. The sequence should be task-oriented and something that would be a lot easier to accomplish with the help of another person: for example, folding the laundry, washing the dishes, painting a wall, mopping a floor, or planting flowers. The designated actor does not tell his partner what task he is performing, but acts out the sequence once or twice. When the partner figures out what is going on, he joins in to help complete the imaginary task.

The first time through the sequence, I suggest the action be pantomimed only, no words or sound. This will enable the actors to focus on refining their action sequence. Follow up by having the partners reverse roles (the second partner initiates an action that the first partner joins). Once each person has had an opportunity to initiate and join in, discuss which one of the sequences worked best. Have each pair choose one sequence and rehearse it again focusing on clearly defined action through pantomime. Once each pair is ready, have them perform the sequence for the rest of the group. This exercise reinforces the notion that acting is a collaborative effort. Focusing on the action allows actors the opportunity to clarify their physical movements before they ever utter a word. This exercise enables the actor to break down action so that it will be more believable to the audience.

Variations

Have the two actors add sound to the sequence. The actors invent sound for such things as hammering a nail, blow-drying one's hair, or cutting a tree down with a chain saw.

Have the two actors do the sequence while saying only one word at a time to each other. This fragmented way of communicating is certainly the way people who know one another very well talk to each other. One word at a time keeps the exercise short, concise, and to the point. Next have them do this with full sentences.

Yet another variation is to have each pair devise a way to put both sequences of action into a single sequence. This will require some inventive decisions on behalf of the partners, but can be very interesting to watch.

Decide on a task to be completed in which the entire group may participate. Possible activities include washing a car, fixing one another's hair for some big social event, or trying to set up a tent at a campsite. Once you have gone through the sequence, try adding sound or words to the action.

Noun Charades

I think just about every student I have ever had enjoyed doing this exercise. Charades are fun to play, and they incorporate many basic acting skills. A spirited game of charades will tap into each participant's ability to gesture, emote, and physicalize action. Noun Charades can be quite engaging and fun to do as well as watch.

Write down on scraps of paper nouns that have broad implications, such as education, music, athletics, art, military, and business. Place these folded pieces of paper into a hat, box, or paper bag for the participants to draw from. As each person draws what he will act out, let him have up to a minute to decide how he will do it. Then he will pantomime a sequence of action that has a clearly defined beginning, middle, and end. Once the sequence of action has been completed, others in the group may guess the word being acted out. Encourage your group to wait until the actor has completed the exercise before they call out their guesses.

Variations

Divide into teams and "compete" against each other. You may want to use more conventional categories such as books, movies, TV programs, phrases, or categories of your own devising.

This exercise can be great fun for all involved. Experiment with other variations that you make up for yourself and the particular needs of your drama group.

Art to Life

Select a number of famous paintings, photographs, or illustrations and bring them in for the group to look at. Either an individual, a pair, or a group will choose one of the pieces to reenact. The actors must decide whether to re-create the action leading up to the moment that is depicted in the painting, photograph, or illustration, or the scene that follows. This exercise prompts the actor to identify with other artists working in different media. A painter or photographer tries to capture the moods, feelings, atmosphere, and characters of life and freeze them in time on a canvas or on film. This exercise gives the actor something to study and analyze and forces him to imagine what motivated the image he sees expressed in a painting or photograph.

Variation

Take a print ad from a catalog, magazine, or newspaper. Ask a group of actors to be your "mannequins." Tell them that you are working on a window display for a department store. When the "display" is complete, the actors/mannequins can come to life and play out a scene, freezing into their original positions at the completion of the exercise. This is an interesting exercise for a group and provides a person who might be interested in directing with an opportunity to work with composition of actors onstage.

Movement to Music

This is an exercise that everyone will enjoy doing. Select four or five segments of instrumental music approximately two to four minutes in length. Divide your group into groups of five to seven people. Have the groups sit together, and play a music selection. Instruct them to listen to the music. Tell the groups to begin discussing how they might act out the music, then play the music again. As they listen to the music a second time, tell them to focus on how the music affects them. Have the groups discuss possible scenarios that have clearly defined beginnings, middles, and ends. Play the music a third, fourth, and even fifth time to allow the groups to rehearse their scenarios. Different groups may interpret the music in similar ways. This is all right, but try to guide the exercise in such a way that there is not too much duplication. Allow each group to perform for the others. Then repeat the exercise with a different selection of music.

Over the years I have discovered that this exercise tends to work best with music that does not contain lyrics. Find a variety of musical selections to use with your group. This is a great exercise to use when working with different ages because it encourages everyone in each group to participate. Generally, someone will emerge as the leader, directing others to perform certain tasks within the exercise. You may find it helpful to appoint someone to oversee the direction each time you do the exercise or just let happen what will happen.

Variations

After you do the exercise with music, try sounds. For example, use a sound effects recording of a thunderstorm, or other environmental sounds such as ocean waves breaking, seagulls, or a train passing. Again, have the groups improvise a scenario to the sounds.

Have members of your group prepare something individually or in groups of two or three for your next meeting.

This exercise taps into the mood and atmosphere that can be created when we introduce sound or music to a production. This can be a compelling exercise to do because it can evoke so many emotions for the actors who perform it.

Inanimate Object Exercise

This imaginative, off-the-wall exercise will tickle the funny bone of everyone participating. The group leader prepares several scraps of paper with a single word or phrase on them, such as peanut butter, maple syrup, newspaper, bubble gum, chair, and frying bacon. The participant selects one of the scraps of paper, and then devises a scenario with a clearly defined beginning, middle, and end around the object. For example, if the object is a clock, the person may decide to change the time or set the alarm. The actor begins by picking the clock up or taking it off the wall. In the middle section, the actor *becomes* the object. In the clock example, the actor uses his arms as the hands of the clock, while making the sounds of the clock ticking. Lastly, the actor becomes himself again and completes the task (of changing the time on the clock). I like this exercise because it taps into a very creative portion of the brain. It normally is very amusing for the participants and teaches the actor how to deal with making transitions onstage.

Prop Exercise

This is another exercise that is imaginative and fun to do with a large group. Have everyone stand in a large circle. Hand one participant a prop with instructions to use the object in a way other than the way it is normally used. For example, if an actor is given a pencil, it could become a rocket on a launchpad that is in a countdown, ready to blast off. If a participant cannot think of anything to do with the object, he passes it on to the next person. Depending on the size of the group, you may pass the object around several times. The group will become more and more inventive. Repeat the exercise using a beach ball, a length of rope, or a piece of cloth. This exercise encourages people to think creatively and quickly.

Variation

You may want to have individuals work on the same exercise with an object of their choosing, giving them a goal of ten, twenty-five, or fifty ways to use the object. This can be given as a project to work on for your next meeting.

Chair Exercise

Ask for a volunteer. Place a chair in front of the group. Instruct the volunteer to make an entrance from either stage right or stage left, cross to the chair, and sit in the chair. Then say to the volunteer, "Show me ten more ways to sit in the chair." Ask the group to watch carefully so that the volunteer does not repeat any position in the process of finding ten additional ways to sit in the chair. After the volunteer has shown ten more ways, the leader may say again, "Show me ten more ways to sit in the chair." The record in my twenty years of using this exercise with students is 200 different ways to sit in the chair. The final instruction for the exercise, when the leader thinks it is time to bring the exercise to closure, is to say to the volunteer, "You have shown us 90 (or whatever number he or she has achieved) ways to sit in the chair. Enter from stage right, cross to the chair, and make a choice about how you will sit in the chair." The volunteer does so, the group applauds, and the volunteer returns to his or her seat.

I adore the simplicity of this exercise and the wonderful things it teaches the group about acting. Everything an actor is directed to do onstage requires the performer to make a choice. If there can be a hundred ways to sit in a chair, then there must be a lot of ways to accomplish any onstage task. The exercise always demands a high level of concentration from the participant. This exercise teaches variety of choices and is simple, yet mind boggling.

When doing this exercise with children, I will frequently reduce the number to five variations and allow each child in the group to show five different ways to sit in the chair. They enjoy the game and will tend to stay with the exercise longer because they know they will be given an opportunity to participate.

Three Station Exercise

Choose three objects that may be used to sit on, such as a small stool, a bench, and a rocking chair. Place the stool down right, the bench center stage, and the rocking chair down left. Have the group line up behind one another in the stage right wing and give the following instructions, "Doing or saying anything you want to as you enter from stage right, you will cross to the stool and sit. You are to play the youngest age you can believably play. You are waiting for someone. When I say 'Next,' the person at the stool will cross to the bench and the next person in line will enter from stage right and cross to the stool. At the second station (the bench) the actor will again be waiting for someone, but will be playing his own age. When the I say 'Next' again, the person at the bench crosses to the rocking chair, and another person enters from stage right and crosses to the stool. At the third station (rocking chair), the participant plays the oldest believable age he can play while again waiting for someone. When the I say 'Next' again, the person in the rocking chair exits stage left and then returns to his seat out front." Continue with the exercise until everyone in the group has had the opportunity to "wait" at the three stations. I like what this exercise teaches actors about making transitions, in this case from one age to the next. It also forces the actor to concentrate and investigate physical methods of depicting age onstage. Almost everyone in the group will excel at playing one of the stations, so the exercise provides a very positive way of working with your actors.

Bake a Cake, Put on Your Makeup, or Build a Bookshelf

This is a great activity to do with children. Have the group pair off. One partner sits in a chair or small stool and the other kneels behind him. The person in the chair puts his hands behind his back and the person on his knees puts his arms around to the front of the person to become that person's "arms" and "hands." The person seated in the chair then describes the step-by-step instructions of how to bake a cake, put on makeup, or build a bookcase, while the person behind tries to perform the tasks described. The results are often hilarious to watch, so do yourself a favor and let each of the pairs perform for one another. My experience with this exercise is that children will beg to do it again and again.

Nonsense Script

This is what is known as a nonsense script or open scene. Give two actors a set of given circumstances. The actors then invent a scene using the words below as the text. An example might be that both Actor One and Actor Two are spies. The words are "code" words. The action could be taking place late at night in a city park. It is very cold outside as the two actors approach one another and sit together on a park bench. This is an exercise that is great fun. Use the lines with as many different situations as you can imagine. Then have the actors themselves invent the circumstances. Write your own nonsense scenes.

Nonsense Script

ONE: HELLO.

TWO: HELLO.

ONE: WELL?

TWO: WELL, WHAT?

ONE: HOW ARE THINGS?

TWO: JUST ABOUT AS USUAL.

ONE: I DIDN'T EXPECT TO FIND YOU HERE.

TWO: BUT YOU HAVE . . . OF COURSE, I COULD SAY THE SAME OF YOU.

ONE: ARE YOU GOING TO BE BUSY FROM NOW UNTIL DINNER?

TWO: NOT EXACTLY . . . NOT BUSY.

ONE: WOULDN'T YOU LIKE TO TALK FOR A LITTLE WHILE?

TWO: I MIGHT. FOR A LITTLE WHILE, ANYWAY.

ONE: RIGHT.

TWO: RIGHT.

Steps for Scene Exploration

As you choose a script to perform, you will need to break down the play into sections or scenes. As you direct the individual scenes, you may find the following information very useful in helping the actors understand what they are saying and doing onstage. This information can be used as a guideline or you may simply pick and choose ideas that may be needed to clarify certain portions of your production.

1. Read the script aloud and talk to the actors about their overall interpretation of the material.

2. Explore the physical environment. Try to be as explicit as possible in describing everything the actors will actually have onstage and things that are not seen, but imagined.

3. Improvise the scene without the script. This is a good technique to use early on when the actors are familiar with the lines but have yet to memorize them.

4. Pantomime the whole scene without using any words.

5. Improvise a past experience from the play. Plays almost always hint at an event that either occurred before the starting point of the play or takes place offstage. As a rehearsal technique, have your actors improvise this experience.

6. Questions and comments—write down everything that comes into your mind concerning the scene. The actors may find it helpful to keep a journal to write down comments and questions they may have for the director. The director may likewise keep a journal of comments and questions to ask the actors.

7. Break down the scene to its physical actions only. Fine-tune all action so the audience will understand everything the actor does onstage.

8. Research and have the actors research music, magazines, photographs, paint-

ings, props, and costumes. This actor/director homework is required to investigate, analyze, and understand any play you may do.

Other Things to Consider in Developing Characterizations Onstage

Have your actors think about the following questions. They may choose to write down their comments in their production journals.

1. What is the relationship between my character and all other characters onstage?
2. What is my character fighting for?
3. Where is the humor in the character I am portraying?
4. What emotions does my character display onstage?
5. How can I make my character three-dimensional?
6. What is the importance of this particular scene? What is the most important moment in this scene?
7. What is the sequence of events in the entire play? How and when does my character fit into the production?
8. Compile a list of adjectives describing what I know about the character I am playing in the production.

Feel free to add additional questions and activities to this list. By answering these questions, the director and the actors will have a clearer idea of what they are trying to communicate to an audience. The key again is to leave no stone unturned and to discover the reasons or the motivations behind why characters say or do certain things in the play. By working through these steps, your actors will begin to develop characters that are believable. The more answers they have about the characters they are creating, the more confident they will become in interpreting the script and understanding the characters they are portraying.

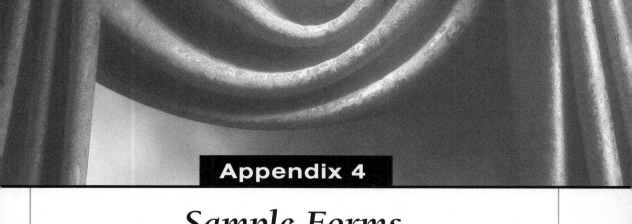

Sample Forms

The purchaser of this book is given permission to reproduce the following pages.

Audition Form

Production _____

Name (As you prefer it to be printed in the theater playbill)

_____

Address _____

Phone number _____

The directors see many people during the audition process. The following are requested purely for the purpose of jogging the memories of the directors and are completely optional.

Age   _____   Voice range _____

Height   _____   Do you play any musical instruments?

Weight   _____   _____

Hair color   _____   _____

Eye color   _____   _____

Previous performance or technical experience (Be concise, list only significant roles and experience):

Time Commitments

Please list all commitments that require your time on a regular basis:

Monday: _____
_____

Tuesday: _____
_____

Wednesday: _____
_____

Thursday: _____
_____

Friday: _____
_____

Saturday: _____
_____

Sunday: _____
_____

If cast in this production, I agree to attend ALL scheduled rehearsals that require my participation. In addition, I agree to accept the responsibilities of preparing and performing any assigned duties given by the director. This includes meeting ALL deadlines for learning material, completing technical assignments, learning lines, blocking, choreography, and songs. Lastly, I agree to participate in the strike of this show immediately following the final performance of the production.

Signature _____

Date _____

Measurement Chart for Women

Production _____

Name _____

Role(s) _____

Height _____   Shoulder to shoulder

Shoe size _____   (front) _____   (back) _____

Weight _____   Shoulder to elbow (bent arm)

Ring size _____   _____

Dress size _____   Shoulder to wrist (bent arm)

Bra size _____   _____

Stocking size _____   Shoulder to wrist (straight arm)

Underpants size _____   _____

Rib cage _____   Neck to shoulder _____

Neck to floor _____   Neck to waist (front) _____

Bust _____   Neck to waist (back) _____

Waist _____   Underarm to waist _____

Outset _____   Around: Biceps _____

Inseam _____   Around: Forearm _____

Hips at fullest part _____   Around: Wrist _____

Around thigh _____   Waist to floor: Front _____

Around calf _____   Waist to floor: Back _____

Around ankle _____   Around head _____

                                 Hat size _____

Waist to knee: Around neck _____

Front _____   Around base of neck _____

Side _____

Back _____

Measurement Chart for Men

Production _____

Name   _____

Role(s)   _____

Height   _____

Shoe size   _____

Weight   _____

Ring size   _____

Suit size: _____

Shirt size: Neck   _____

Shirt size: Sleeve _____

Trousers: Waist   _____

Trousers: Inseam   _____

Waist   _____

Outset   _____

Inseam   _____

Hips at fullest part _____

Around thigh   _____

Around calf   _____

Around ankle   _____

Waist to knee:

Front   _____

Side   _____

Back   _____

Shoulder to shoulder

(front) _____   (back) _____

Shoulder to elbow (bent arm)

_____

Shoulder to wrist (bent arm)

_____

Shoulder to wrist (straight arm)

_____

Neck to shoulder   _____

Neck to waist (front) _____

Neck to waist (back) _____

Underarm to waist   _____

Around: Biceps   _____

Around: Forearm   _____

Around: Wrist   _____

Waist to floor: Front _____

Waist to floor: Back _____

Around head   _____

Hat size   _____

Around neck   _____

Around base of neck   _____

Light Cue Sheet

Production _____

Lt. Q#	Script Page	Dimmers	Level	Count

Property List

Production _____

Act One Presets:

Act Two Presets:

Call Sheet

Production: _____

Date: _____

Call:

Business:

Costume Plot

Production ———————————————————————

Actor's name ———————————————————————

Character ———————————————————————

Act ———————————————————————

Costume:

Accessories:

Makeup Face Map

Title of production _____

Date of production _____

Actor's name   _____

Role(s) played   _____

Analysis of character:

Age of character:

Climate in which character lives and works:

Race of character:

Health of character:

Environment in which character lives and works:

Style of production:

Period of time in which production is set:

Indicate the areas on this face where makeup is to be applied:

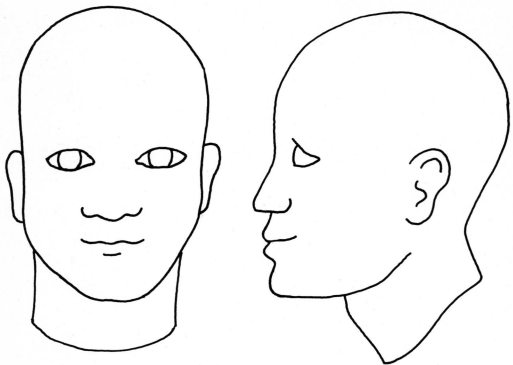

Notes relating to makeup colors and methods of application:

Mouth:

Eyes:

Forehead:

Chin:

Nose:

Cheeks:

Hair:

Richard Major is a professor of theater at Milligan College in Tennessee, where he also chairs the department of Performing, Visual, and Communicative Arts. A member of Actors' Equity Association, Major is an accomplished actor, director, and teacher of acting. With nearly one hundred acting and voice over roles to his credit, and a similar number of directing credits, Major has worked in a variety of professional capacities with church groups, community outreach organzations, and educational and professional theaters throughout the southeast United States.

Richard Major lives in Johnson City, Tennessee, with his wife, Karen, and their children, Will and Shannon.